LOVE, HONOR & FORGIVE

Bill & Pam Farrel

A Guide for Married Couples

InterVarsity Press

Downers Grove. Illinois

InterVarsity Press
P.O. Box 1400, Downers Grove, IL 60515
World Wide Web: www.ivpress.com
E-mail: mail@ivpress.com

InterVarsity Press® is the book-publishing division of InterVarsity Christian Fellowship/USA®, a
student movement active on campus at hundreds of universities, colleges and schools of nursing in
the United States of America, and a member movement of the International Fellowship of Evangelical
Students. For information about local and regional activities, write Public Relations Dept.,
InterVarsity Christian Fellowship/USA, 6400 Schroeder Rd., P.O. Box 7895, Madison, WI
53707-7895.

In "God's Statement of Love to Us" all Scripture passages, unless otherwise noted, are quoted from the
International Children's Bible, New Century Version, copyright 1986, 1988, 1994 by Word
Publishing, Dallas, TX 75234. Used by permission.

All other Scripture quotations, unless otherwise indicated, are taken from the Holy Bible, New
International Version®. NIV®. Copyright ©1973, 1978, 1984 by International Bible Society. Used by
permission of Zondervan Publishing House. All rights reserved.

Cover photograph: SuperStock

ISBN 0-8308-2227-5

Printed in the United States of America ∞

Library of Congress Cataloging-in-Publication Data

Farrel, Bill, 1959-
    Love, honor & forgive
       p. cm.
    Includes bibliographical references.
    ISBN 0-8308-2227-5 (pbk. alk. paper)
      1. Spouses—Religious life. 2. Forgiveness—Religious aspects—Christianity. I. Title:
Love, honor & forgive. II. Farrel, Pam, 1959- III. Title.
BV4596.M3 F367 2000
248.8'44—dc 21
                                               99-055903

18	17	16	15	14	13	12	11	10	9	8	7	6	5	4	3	2

14	13	12	11	10	09	08	07	06	05	04	03

In loving memory of Pam's father,
Billy R. Rogers.
Forgiveness gives love wings
and hope springs anew.

God will "bestow on them a crown of
beauty instead of ashes,
the oil of gladness instead of mourning,
and a garment of praise
instead of a spirit of despair."

ISAIAH 61:3

CONTENTS

One

What Is There to Forgive?

The air was tense. Everyone could sense that something was wrong, but no one was talking about it. The family members were busy with their prescribed tasks. The table was being set and dinner was being cooked while the children were playing. The strong handsome man in the recliner could take the stilted silence no more. Clearing his throat, he stood to his feet.

"Could I have everyone's attention? Could everyone please stop what they are doing and come to the living room?"

Slowly they all filed in—his teenage children, the in-laws, their friends and his wife. They had come for a dinner party after church, but this didn't seem like a party at all. Wringing his hands, Sean stood in the center of the room. The strain on his face was apparent to everyone. They all just stared and waited.

Sean stood with shoulders slumped like the Thinker statue. Then, taking a deep breath and pulling himself up straight, he began, "I'm glad you're all here. I know this isn't what you came for, but it has to be done. I want to tell you all how sorry I am. I have failed my children. I haven't been there for them. My drinking has caused this family great damage. And, honey . . ."

He looked to his battle-weary wife who was beautiful but aged beyond her years by the strain she'd been living under.

"Honey, I haven't been there for you."

Sean broke down. Tears tumbled down his cheeks and off his square jaw.

"Please forgive me. I was wrong."

He looked around the room at the eyes that were fixed on him with a mixture of relief and disbelief.

"All of you. I am sorry. Please forgive me. If you can, please pray for me. Please forgive me."

With that, Sean fell to his knees and wept uncontrollably with his face buried in his hands.

I'm sorry. Please forgive me. Those words are difficult to hear and even more difficult to speak. How can a relationship be repaired and restored when the water under the bridge has become a torrential flood of hurt, wounds, angry words and actions? Is there hope to be found in a relationship when both the husband and wife feel hopeless?

Sean and his wife are one of the many couples who have discovered that forgiveness can heal any situation. Every couple has experienced those times when, against their better judgment, they have needlessly hurt one another. Many couples have brutalized their relationships with decisions that defy any logical explanation. No amount of apologies can erase the devastating words. No amount of pleading can dull the ache of having been rejected. No promises can convince you that your spouse will not violate the relationship again. When your relationship simply needs an adjustment, good communication skills or a renewed commitment to romance may restore its value in your heart. But when the relationship has been cheapened by the darkness of human nature, only heartfelt, courageous forgiveness can bring healing to your heart and arouse new hope for your relationship.

In the pages that follow, you will explore the path of forgiveness. You will be exposed to the prevalent misconceptions that overshadow the power of forgiveness. You will be confronted with the obstacles that cripple people's ability to forgive. And you will meet people who have experienced the transforming power of forgiveness firsthand. The names of many of them have been changed to protect their privacy, but their stories are real. You will discover that forgiveness is a process rather than an event and that healing unfolds over time. You will also be challenged to accept that God intends to redeem *any and every* bad circumstance of your marriage if you are willing to surround it with forgiveness.

Sweeping for Land Mines

You got married because you believed you were compatible together as a couple. Since that first step, however, you have come to the haunting realization that he is impossible to live with. You have become overwhelmed with the steady list of expectations she lays out for you. The love of your dreams has disappeared in a haze of disappointment. It is as if the open field of possibilities in your marriage was booby trapped with land mines and you have stepped on most of them.

The rigors of everyday life will take a toll on even the best of marriage relationships. Often the only way to handle the frustration of being hurt by the one you love is to master the process of forgiveness. In this chapter we will look at some of the common obstacles that create hurt feelings in love relationships and isolate a husband and wife from each other. Some of these obstacles are irritations of everyday living, while others are intense circumstances in life that significantly impact our ability to cope with the responsibility of intimacy.

Miscommunication

I (Bill) was anxiously looking forward to being present at the birth of our second son, Zachery. In order to be admitted, I had to attend classes at the hospital that explained the procedure of caesarian birth and the role of the coach. The appointed day came and I was running late. I was tied up at work and I knew Pam would be getting anxious. Sure enough, she called me at the office.

"Hi, Pam. I know I'm late but I am leaving the office now. I'll see you at home."

"No, wait," Pam interjected. "Linda is going to watch Brock, so meet me at Linda's house."

"OK," I said. "I'll meet you at Linda's."

Triumphant that I had dodged a bullet, I headed off to meet her at Linda's. Driving up, I was surprised that Pam was not there yet. I figured she'd had trouble getting our two-year-old out the door, and so I sat in my car and patiently waited, reviewing my responsibilities for the rest of the day. After a few minutes, Linda came out and said I had a phone call from Pam.

"Where *are* you, Bill?"

"I'm at Linda's, where are you?"

"I'm at Linda L.'s house waiting for you!"

Oh no! I had assumed Pam meant Linda B.'s house, because she had done a lot of babysitting for us. I could hear the panic in Pam's voice; she was beginning to doubt we would make it to the class. I said I would hurry over to where she was.

"No, that will take too much time. Just meet me at the hospital."

"OK—meet you at the hospital."

As she was driving to the birthing center, a building next to the hospital, Pam was thinking about what she had told me. *He knows we need to meet at the birthing center, doesn't he? I know I said "hospital" but he knows better.* As she passed the hospital on her way to the birthing center, she saw my car in the hospital parking lot. *There he is. He is such a guy! He never can keep the details straight.*

We finally got to the class that allowed me to be at the birth of our second son, but the events of that day were a disaster. We had so miscommunicated with each other that there was no way to rectify the situation. The only recourse for restoring peace in our relationship was forgiveness.

Misunderstandings

Sometimes the tension in our relationships is caused by a very sincere misunderstanding. You were trying your hardest, and your efforts backfired. You attempted to make things better, but you got deeper in a hole. It is possible to get a long way off track before you realize it.

During his visit to Korea, Governor Mike Leavitt of Utah was relaxing in the VIP lounge of the Seoul Airport, awaiting his flight to Japan. At the same moment, his press secretary, Vicki Varela, was being told at the ticket counter that she had no ticket.

After she insisted she had to make the flight because she was with a U.S. governor, an American embassy aide intervened. Vicki got a standby ticket and boarded just before takeoff. Regaining her composure, she went to the front of the plane to tell Leavitt of her adventure. He was not there. She later found out that the governor had been bumped by an urgent standby passenger. It was Vicki.[1]

Vicki was trying to do the right thing. She wanted her boss to succeed, and she thought her efforts were helping him to be more efficient. Instead, she was making life more difficult for Governor Leavitt. In the same way, we often make life more difficult for the ones we love because our well-intentioned efforts create a misunderstanding rather than a solution.

Irresponsibility

At other times, our relationships are disrupted by a failure to keep up with our responsibilities. It may be a minor issue such as Rosida Porter of South Solon, Ohio, reports in the following incident:

> When I was in high school, musical car horns were popular. My mother's deluxe model played the first line of 48 different songs. But when it was extremely cold, the horn sometimes developed a short and played on its own. I urged Mom to take it out of our car, but she refused to get rid of it. That is, until the cold winter afternoon that Mom and Dad attended a graveside funeral service for an elderly aunt. As they were pulling out of the cemetery, the horn blared the first stanza of "We're in the Money." I never heard the horn again.[2]

Sometimes, however, it may be a habit of irresponsibility that dramatically affects your marriage and family relationships. Listen as

Sean recounts how his drinking led to mistrust.

> Rita had to choose to forgive my years of isolating and abandoning her.
> Years of not keeping my word. I can remember the biggest change I
> saw at first was that I wanted to re-earn trust in her eyes and the eyes
> of the kids. The next Friday night I was at a football game, and one of
> my sons paged me and added a 9-1-1 to the end. When I immediately
> left the game to call him, he was surprised. When I told my friend what
> the page was about, he said, "Why the 9-1-1? That wasn't an emer-
> gency." That's when it hit me. For years I had ignored pages—even real
> emergency ones, like the time my mother-in-law had to leave my wife,
> just home from the hospital, alone with our five-year-old daughter. I
> was supposed to go home and care for them. I never went home, and I
> didn't answer their pages. Instead I went to a bar and got drunk. So my
> family was used to my betraying their trust. Even 9-1-1 pages hadn't
> worked in the past, so now I was determined to be faithful in the every-
> day little things to reearn trust.[3]

The plain truth is that it is impossible for two human beings to live
together for any length of time and not hurt each other. All too often
life gets in the way of living. If the struggles of marriage were isolated
to the minor irritations that come along with being imperfect, we
would probably all have great marriages. But minor irritations can
grow into major problems—and major infractions can break your
heart. Sometimes the mistreatment you have experienced from others
in your past creates patterns in your own behavior that hinder your
current relationship. If any of the following destructive forces have
invaded your marriage, only forgiveness will open the door to healing.

Traumatic Events in Your Life

When your marriage is being disrupted by circumstances outside your
personal relationship, things can get pretty confusing. Life is unpredictable, and it can change at any moment. In the confusion of the
trauma, couples often turn on one another in an attempt to vent painful
emotions or to find some perspective that makes sense.

The Old Testament tells the story of a man named Job (rhymes with *robe*). Job and his wife were living an incredibly successful life. Business was booming. His family was strong and healthy. His relationship with his wife was satisfying. And his reputation in the community was without equal. In fact, "He was the greatest man among all the people of the East" (Job 1:3).

Then, through no fault of his own, life dramatically changed for Job. God had confidence in him and entered him in a contest. God negotiated with Satan a plan to show how sufficient faith is in the lives of believers. "Have you considered my servant Job? There is no one on earth like him; he is blameless and upright, a man who fears God and shuns evil" (Job 1:8).

To prove the point, God gave Satan permission to traumatize Job through the loss of his wealth and his children. Amazingly, Job took the loss in stride. His response appears almost superhuman to us as he uses this tragedy to initiate praise for God. "'Naked I came from my mother's womb, and naked I will depart. The Lord gave and the Lord has taken away; may the name of the Lord be praised.' In all this, Job did not sin by charging God with wrongdoing" (Job 1:21-22).

Job's integrity infuriated Satan, so he renegotiated with God for permission to strike Job with a painful illness. God reluctantly but confidently gave Satan permission, and the tragedy in Job's life escalated. At this point Job's wife could take no more. She had been a spectator to the dismantling of her life and the destruction of her heart. Job's calmness in the midst of this hurricane only served to intensify her anguish. In anger she lashed out, "Are you still holding on to your integrity? Curse God and die!" (Job 2:9).

Although Job remained strong through this incredible tragedy, his wife suffered great emotional and spiritual wounds through the loss of her children and her financial security. She was never going to get her kids back, and she would never be able to erase the trauma of these events. Out of her pain, she said things that would only serve to spread the anguish into her relationship with God and into her marriage. Her heart still needed to be healed. Only the forgiveness of God and Job could give her a second chance at finding peace.

Abuse in Your Background

As a young girl, Sarah was often neglected and ignored. As a result, she developed a dull sense of discernment. She had a hard time recognizing safe people and would gravitate toward anyone who would give her attention. Marvin was her favorite uncle. At the age of seven she loved the playful way he welcomed her, and she was amazed that he would get down on the floor and play games with her when all the other adults were too busy talking to notice her. When Marvin suggested a new game that only he and she would ever know about, she was intrigued. She remembers feeling funny about the way Marvin touched her, outside her clothes first, then progressing to fondling her genitals, but she trusted Marvin and so she went along with it.

When the game progressed to the point that they were both naked, she finally sensed that this had to stop. She told her parents about the games. She said he touched her in the places where her bathing suit covered.

But her parents' response was less than helpful. "Honey, he would *not* do that. You must be making things up. You probably just misunderstood the game. We all know you have a very active imagination."

Even though the family never confronted Marvin, the games stopped, so Sarah put it out of her mind and got on with her life. She was vaguely aware during high school that her immoral choices might not be good, but she reasoned, *Everyone is doing it, so what's the big deal?* She was also periodically nagged by the fact that she only dated when she could be in control of the relationship. She figured it was better that way. She wasn't going to marry any of these boys anyway, and it was better to be in control and not get hurt.

When she finally met Anthony, she was ready to settle down and have a family life. She respected Anthony because he was easygoing but was not afraid to make decisions. She felt that he would be kind to her but would also have the strength to give their lives direction.

For the most part their marriage was working well. She noticed some things she didn't like, but she didn't think they were very abnormal.

The atmosphere in her heart started to change, though, shortly after her oldest daughter's sixth birthday. She was plagued by heavy moods of sadness and anxiety. She felt a desperate need to protect her children and became more demanding of her husband. He, of course, felt as if he had lost his wife and been given an ogre in her place. She tried to tell herself that it was not a big deal, but she didn't know *what it was* that wasn't a big deal! Her sadness progressed into apathy and finally into full-scale depression. The whole process came to a crisis point on her daughter's seventh birthday when the memories of her uncle suddenly flooded her heart with intense pain.

If anyone even *thought* about doing to her daughter what Marvin had done to her, she would take swift and decisive action to protect her daughter. Somehow, though, she couldn't come to her own rescue. She felt helpless and used. Grief set in and dragged her into inactivity. When she wasn't overwhelmed by sadness, she was blaming Anthony. Her problems in life had been caused by a man, and he was a man.

Her grieving lasted most of that year, as she shed an abundance of tears during periods of introspection that lasted days at a time. She finally grew tired of being depressed and began looking for answers. When she heard that she needed to start by forgiving Marvin, she recoiled in revulsion.

"I can never forgive that man for the things he did to me! He doesn't deserve it."

As she wrestled with the issue, she finally realized that she needed to forgive her uncle *for her sake, not his.* Freedom to forgive developed when she realized she could forgive her uncle and still be adamant that his behavior was wrong. She didn't have to be bitter toward him to maintain her conviction about how wrong it is to abuse children. The willingness to forgive her uncle eased the tension toward her husband. As bitterness was disarmed, the need to vent her pain on Anthony was diminished. Also, the realization that this was a violation by her uncle and not a general characteristic of all men enabled her to take a new look at Anthony and rebuild her trust in him. Abuse had stolen her innocence, but bitterness had stolen intimacy. Her innocence cannot be recovered, but forgiveness can redeem it and restore her loving relationship with Anthony.

Unhealthy Family Patterns

Families use all kinds of unhealthy tactics to motivate one another. Guilt, manipulation, sarcasm, unrealistic expectations and constant criticism are examples of learned habits that families pass on from generation to generation. Because these tactics are inherently negative, they cause damage in those who learn them. Since these influences become part of who we are, we take them into our marriages and punish our spouses with the family weapons.

When Jason was growing up, he often heard his dad say degrading things to his mom. "You're too stupid to figure this out." "You look like a whore; change your clothes." "Your make-up is put on like paint—go back and get it right." "You are gaining too much weight. If you want to look like a cow, maybe you can sleep out on the grass." Jason didn't like hearing his dad use these words, but that was his dad.

As he grew older, Jason became aware that his dad was using the same approach with him. In high school, Jason and his dad had a falling out because of his dad's abusive judgments. "You play football like a woman. When are you going to really hit someone?" "You dress like a wimp." "You should get a job, because you're too stupid to go to college." Jason told himself he was never going to be like his dad.

Then he met Rachel. She was beautiful, sensitive and soft-spoken. She too had grown up with a hot-tempered father. Together they decided they were going to be different. They weren't going to yell and scream—and they don't. But Jason has carried along his father's sarcasm and critical spirit. Rachel thinks to herself, *If he loves me, why does he call me stupid? If we were going to do things differently, why is he so demanding and never satisfied? Why does he say such mean things?* Jason and Rachel love each other deeply and want to have a workable relationship, but

Jason's acquired skill of meanness drives Rachel away.

Here is the crucial factor: Jason will never remove his dad's influence until he learns to forgive his dad. If this negative influence is not courageously redeemed, Jason will continue to tear down Rachel's sense of value until she becomes convinced that she can never satisfy Jason. If, on the other hand, Jason recognizes the destructive bent that has arisen within himself, learned from his father, he can apply forgiveness and free himself to grow beyond it. He and Rachel will then be able to create a home that is substantially different from the homes they grew up in.

Violations of the Marriage Relationship

Sean, the man from the beginning of this chapter, didn't start out wanting to abandon Rita emotionally, but that is what happened.

He had hit the pavement running in his career. He worked long hours, got promotions and provided well for his family. But the stress of this productivity was high, and he found that a couple of drinks after work helped him wind down. The combination of hard work and alcohol dulled his senses toward Rita so that she was gradually shut out of his life. The intimacy they had shared early in their relationship was replaced with isolation and independence. They were not upset with each other, but they were not really interested in each other either. Thus the stage was set for trouble.

When the rising costs of raising the kids strained their budget, Sean and Rita decided to take a boarder. Financially it seemed to be a good decision, but emotionally it turned out to be a disaster. The new tenant was a sympathetic young man with time to talk. In the absence of Sean's support and attention, Rita began opening up to this new man in their life. She never intended to get attached, but over time the attraction was irresistible.

"My drinking after work kept me at the bar with the guys and not home with Rita," recalls Sean. "I was oblivious to what was going on under my own roof! It wasn't until one of Rita's relatives came to stay that Rita was confronted with her new relationship. The relative saw what was happening and let Rita know that he knew."

Sean and Rita were catapulted from denial to disaster. Should Sean be upset about Rita's affair? If he confronted her with the affair, would Rita justify her affair because of his drinking and absenteeism? What should he do about his drinking and his overcommitment to work? In a case like this there are no easy solutions. The first action to take is to forgive. They had both violated the relationship, and they both needed to return to the starting line where God could meet them and give them a new race to run.

Forgiveness Is the First Step

Forgiveness is the first step to healing the past. Forgiveness is also the first step to healthy relationships in the present. None of us can ignore it. We choose either to master forgiveness or to be mastered by bitterness. There are a number questions we must ask ourselves up front to prepare to master forgiveness.

Whom do you want to have the greatest influence in your life? Whoever has the greatest emotional tie to your heart will make the biggest difference in your life. One of the strongest emotions on earth is bitterness. The Bible refers to bitterness as a root that will grow until it invades your entire inner life (Heb 12:15). Studies show that we tend to become like the people we focus on. If you are focused on the people who have hurt you, you will become like them. We cannot, however, just choose to not think about them. We must transform our thinking (Rom 12:2) and replace them with role models and patterns of growth that lead us to healthy patterns of living (Heb 13:7).

Are you willing to trade in revenge for freedom? If you are going to master forgiveness, you must be willing to put judgment into the hands of God and not worry about whether those who have wronged you get what they deserve. You must have a desire in your heart to find the freedom that leads you to growth and new horizons. If you have a need buried in your heart for people to pay for what they have done to you, you will be blocked from the path that leads to a life of new possibilities.

Are you willing to look ahead? Bitterness is always focused on the past.

If you want to let go of the past and move on with your life, you must be willing to forgive so you can focus on the bright future God has planned for you. If you refuse to forgive, you will be locked in the past and your life will be defined by the negative things that have happened to you. You will become dissatisfied with present relationships and exhausted from trying to drag along the anchor of your past. Hope is in the future. The future is full of possibilities and opportunities.

What motivation do you want to have in life? The greatest motivation in life is love, but love is seriously threatened by bitterness. Bitterness will overwhelm every other desire and take over the life of its victim. It will not share its throne for very long. If left unchecked, it will systematically take over every area of life and make all other motivations subordinate to itself. Only forgiveness will neutralize bitterness and open your heart to the love of Christ for you and your loved ones.

Are you willing to accept help? Only the Holy Spirit can look at the core of who you are and show you the truth about whether you have truly forgiven. You must be willing to ask him to search your heart— and then you must be ready to respond to his leading. Psalm 139:23-24 poignantly says, "Search me, O God, and know my heart; test me and know my anxious thoughts. See if there is any offensive way in me, and lead me in the way everlasting." If you have a habit of withholding forgiveness, then you need a new start. You need new information. What you already know is not sufficient to lead you out of the habit. If it was, you wouldn't still be holding resentment in your heart. You need help in developing new ways of thinking and a new approach to life that will lead you in a new direction. Working harder on what is not working will not make it work. You need the Holy Spirit as a source of information and ability beyond what you can accomplish on your own.

Focus on the Heart

Heavenly Father, help me to be stronger than my past. "Search me, O God, and know my heart; test me and know my anxious thoughts. See if there is any offensive way in me, and lead me in the way everlasting."

A Step Toward Love

Ask yourself the following questions as a way to discover how ready you are to forgive:

☐ Whom do you want to have the greatest influence in your life?
☐ Are you willing to trade in revenge for freedom?
☐ Are you willing to look ahead?
☐ What motivation do you want to have in life?
☐ Are you willing to accept help?

Two

Why Should I Forgive?

S usan *grew up in a home where alcohol and anger mixed together to* make for an unstable environment. Her mom and dad often went to the bar together, leaving the home under the supervision of her older sister. They often came home and continued the fight that had started at the bar.

"Why were you flirting with every other woman there?" her mom would be screaming as they came in the front door.

"I wasn't flirting with them. How come you have to ruin every good time we have?" Dad would shoot back.

"It wasn't me who ruined it. I went to have fun with you, but it's obvious you would rather be with someone else."

"If I wanted to be with someone else I'd just do it. Don't flatter yourself, there are better fish in the ocean."

"Oh yeah, well, I could have a better man than you. Maybe you want me to be with someone else so you can be free. Well, you are not free. You're with me."

"Right now I wish I wasn't. You are so hard to live with. No one could be happy with you."

At this point, the argument would usually got out of hand and Mom would throw something at Dad. Dad would react and Mom would throw more things. The day Dad left was the day he charged at Mom during one of these fights and took a plate in the forehead. He got so angry when the plate hit him that he took a swing at his wife and connected just above her right eye. When he looked at her lying on the ground with blood running down her cheek, he knew things had gone too far. He left the house and never returned.

Susan was fourteen at the time. She spent the rest of her teen years without a father in her home and with a flood of questions in her heart. *Why did my dad have to leave? Where is God in all of this? Are there any good men left in the world?* Her lack of answers to these questions sent her heart spinning with disappointment and anger. She grew increasingly angry with her dad for abandoning her and her mom at a critical time of life. She became furious over the lack of respect that teenage boys were showing her and her friends. She regretted the anger she felt toward her mom for her bouts with alcohol and for her limitless self-pity. The end result was an undercurrent of anger that permeated Susan's life. It wasn't obvious to everyone who knew her because it wasn't always on the surface. But when someone got close to Susan and put her in a position of vulnerability, she would erupt. The risk of trusting another individual was too big a challenge for her and triggered the hurt inflicted upon her by her father.

Bob loves Susan and wants to encourage her but has become increasingly frustrated with her. Every time he gets close to her something strange happens. She lashes out if he does anything remotely resembling her dad. She makes outrageous statements about Bob being selfish and "just like every other man," even though he has been a very attentive husband. Their time with friends is often interrupted by angry outbursts from Susan when she perceives a woman being treated with a lack of respect. For Bob and Susan to find the intimacy they both desire, Susan needs to forgive her parents, and Bob needs to forgive Susan.

Forgiveness is a gritty process. It challenges us to be mature at the deepest levels of our lives—and so there are many barriers to the fulfillment of forgiveness. In order to be a person who defeats bitterness, your reasons for forgiving must be more compelling than your reasons for holding on to the pain.

Your Kids Need You to Forgive

"Kids, please come into the living room, Mom and Dad have something to tell you." Too often these days, the news Mom and Dad have to tell the children is that they are getting a divorce.

In the January 27, 1997, issue of *Newsweek*, some startling statistics were cited by Tom Morganthau: "Half of all children will witness the breakup of their parents' marriage. Half of these children will also go on to see the breakup of a parent's second marriage. Kids in single-parent and blended families are twice as likely to drop out of school and are at a higher risk for teen pregnancy."

Judith S. Wallerstein and Sandra Blakslee conducted a study in which they followed sixty families through the process of divorce. Family members were examined eighteen months after the divorce and then at five- and ten-year intervals. You would think that after so many years, much of the struggle would have subsided. But "incredibly, one-half of the women and one-third of the men are still intensely angry at their former spouse, despite the passage of ten years. Because their feelings have not changed, anger has become an ongoing, and sometimes dominant, presence in their children's lives as well."[1] "A third of the women and a quarter of the men . . . feel that life is unfair, disappointing, and lonely."[2]

It appears that unresolved anger becomes a family legacy in these cases as "in this study . . . almost half of the children entered adulthood as worried, underachieving, self-depreciating, and sometimes angry young men and women."[3] In addition, Wallerstein and Blakslee conclude that "by avoiding our task [of maintaining our commitment to marriage], we have unintentionally placed the primary burden of coping with family change onto the children. To state it plainly, we are allowing our children to bear the psychological, economic and moral brunt of divorce."[4]

So before you decide that you cannot forgive your spouse and that divorce is the only answer, consider the impact on the children. Often, when marriages are in trouble, Bill and I have talked with the children affected by impending divorce. Here are a few expressions from the hearts of these children:

"I never want to get married. Love always hurts."—age twelve

"I learned that hate doesn't just shut Mom out of Dad's heart, it shuts everyone out—even me."—high-school senior

"You have to be bad to get Dad's attention. He used to come to my games, my activities at school, but he hates Mom so much, now he only comes when I'm in trouble."—junior-high boy

"God doesn't answer prayers. I prayed Mommy and Daddy wouldn't get a divorce, but they did anyway."—age six

"Mom would rather have sex with her boyfriend and leave me alone to babysit than live in a nice house with Dad. I hate this!"—age eleven

"Dad would rather choose a new TV and a new girlfriend and a new family instead of choosing me."—age seven

"Why won't Dad play by the rules? The rule is: you say 'I love you.' You get married and you live together happily ever after with your kids. That's the rule. He wants me to play by the rules and not cheat but he cheated, whatever that means. Now my Mom cries all the time and even when I hug her she won't stop."—age nine

"Please pray for me, another family stole my daddy."—age seven

"Please tell me who to choose. I don't want to have to choose who to love. I heard Dad say to Mommy that he'd take me and she could take my sissy. But I want my sissy with me. Why won't they just love each other so me and sissy can be together?"—age six

"Dad used to love Mommy, but he doesn't now. I hope he won't 'used to love' me too."—age five

---

According to a recent *Focus on the Family* radio program, divorced children have their greatest struggles five years after a divorce.[5] If you think things are bad now, think down the road, picture those kids, then call a pastor or Christian counselor for help—*one more time.*

Your Spirit Needs You to Forgive

The Bible teaches us that a lack of forgiveness will give Satan an advantage in our lives in his efforts to deceive. The apostle Paul says,

> And what I have forgiven—if there was anything to forgive—I have forgiven in the sight of Christ for your sake, in order that Satan might not outwit us. For we are not unaware of his schemes. (2 Cor 2:10-11)

Satan desires access into our lives, and so he schemes to stretch the limits of his authority by finding an advantage in us. These advantages are usually subtle and invisible to the casual observer. It is not until you are looking for them that you notice their presence. They start off as negative influences, such as a lack of forgiveness, that evil spirits then exploit in order to keep the lives of believers off balance. The goal is to disrupt the godly influence of believers and render them useless in the process of helping others find the power and hope of eternal life.

The Bible goes on to say that unresolved anger can give Satan access to our soul through "footholds." " 'In your anger do not sin': Do not let the sun go down while you are still angry, and do not give the devil a foothold" (Eph 4:26-27). A helpful way to picture the effects of a foothold is to imagine your life like a room. Inside the room, if you have received Christ as your personal savior, are you and the Holy Spirit. The room has many doors and windows that can be opened or closed. Each of these doors and windows represents an area where a foothold could be developed. It is your choice whether the door or window is open or not. Let's say that one of the windows is open because of bitterness. Outside that window is a demon who is trying to distract you. Imagine trying to carry on your life inside the room while the demon is making faces at you or saying obnoxious things to you. It would be distracting, to say the least.

The strange part of this is that we get used to the visitors. We learn to adapt to the open doors and windows. The extra noise gives a sense of camaraderie and companionship. The foothold is never identified as a negative spiritual influence, so there is no panic or disturbance over its presence. When forgiveness is embraced and the footholds associated with the bitterness are shut down, loneliness can hit like a wave. The familiar spiritual influence is gone, and a disquieting silence takes its place. In order to achieve long-lasting forgiveness, you must be willing to live with the silence. It requires learning a new approach to life—one that has a single source of spiritual input rather than the noisy world of bitterness.

Your Future Needs You to Forgive

She had ascended in her career so that she commanded the respect of her colleagues as well as her subordinates. Her reputation was flawless and her influence dramatic. As a result, her confidence was high, and she inspired confidence in everyone who had contact with her. Her name was Miriam.

She was present when the nation of Israel crossed the Red Sea under the leadership of Moses. She witnessed the miraculous rescue of her country and the dramatic demise of the Egyptian army as the horses and riders were drowned by the collapse of the rushing waters. In her position as a prophetess, she was inspired by God to lead the women in praise and celebration.

> Then Miriam the prophetess, Aaron's sister, took a tambourine in her hand, and all the women followed her, with tambourines and dancing. Miriam sang to them:
>
> Sing to the LORD,
>   for he is highly exalted.
> The horse and its rider
>   he has hurled into the sea. (Ex 15:20-21)

Miriam was enjoying her success and could feel the power of God working in her life. Things had never been better. But the challenge of the human experience got the better of her. As her fame and impact grew, so did her envy toward her more famous brother, Moses. Moses was not the kind of leader Miriam thought he should be. She questioned his decisions and silently despised his leadership style. As a result, a root of bitterness began to grow.

When Moses chose a wife from the tribe of Cush, Miriam concluded he had made an inappropriate choice, and she started a campaign of grumbling. The grumbling, however, was not limited to his choice of a wife. It stretched into an evaluation of his entire ministry. "Miriam and Aaron began to talk against Moses because of his Cushite wife, for he had married ɛ Cushite. 'Has the Lord spoken only through Moses?' they asked. 'Hasn't he also spoken through us?'" (Num 12:1-2).

Many women have the same struggles with their husbands that Miriam had with her brother. Your husband may not be doing anything wrong, but he isn't doing the things you think he should. His leadership style is not satisfying to you. In your opinion, he is ignoring issues that are vital to the health and security of your family. He is insensitive to the needs you feel most acutely, and he is far too passive in his decision-making to inspire any confidence in your heart.

We hear this kind of murmuring most often when wives are commenting on the spiritual leadership of their husbands. We hear statements such as these: "My husband is not much of a spiritual leader." "I wish my husband would take the lead in our family." "If my husband were more enthusiastic about Christ, our marriage would be so much better." It is true that many husbands are ignoring their God-given responsibilities when it comes to their families. Husbands often value the physical appearance of their wives and their own personal comfort above more important qualities such as integrity and character. But it is just as true that many husbands who work hard to provide, who spend plenty of time with their children and whose families are faithfully involved in a local church are criticized because they don't have much style. Their wives want a man who is spectacular rather than steady, flamboyant rather than faithful, outstanding rather than ordinary. If you are not careful, your expectations for your spouse will be transformed into bitterness in your heart, and, like Miriam, you may inappropriately express your dissatisfaction.

When Miriam spoke out, "the LORD heard this" (Num 12:2). Now it was a spiritual problem. Bitterness is never just a matter of human relationships. Bitterness in the heart will always short-circuit a relationship with Christ. The Lord heard what Miriam said, and he got involved.

> At once the LORD said to Moses, Aaron and Miriam, "Come out to the Tent of Meeting, all three of you." So the three of them came out. Then the LORD came down in a pillar of cloud; he stood at the entrance to the Tent and summoned Aaron and Miriam. When both of them stepped forward, he said, "Listen to my words:
>
> When a prophet of the LORD is among you,
>   I reveal myself to him in visions,
>   I speak to him in dreams.
> But this is not true of my servant Moses;
>   he is faithful in all my house.
> With him I speak face to face,
>   clearly and not in riddles;
>   he sees the form of the LORD.
> Why then were you not afraid
>   to speak against my servant Moses?"
> The anger of the LORD burned against them, and he left them.
>
> When the cloud lifted from above the Tent, there stood Miriam—leprous, like snow. (Num 12:4-10)

Miriam's success had been displaced by a huge setback in life because bitterness had crippled her spiritually.

A married couple is a partnership of two talented individuals. At different times and during different phases of life, God will choose for your spouse's potential to shine while you take a supportive role. As you become aware of your own potential, you may struggle with being patient. When you move ahead of God and think you should have the opportunity that belongs to the other person, God often frustrates your plans. Your confident attempt to get something done becomes your undoing. It isn't that you *can't* do it. It is just that it isn't yours to do — or maybe it is just not your time. When this level of competition characterizes a marriage, humility and forgiveness are the only paths to healing.

Fortunately for Miriam, Moses was a man of humility and forgiveness. He sought the Lord on Miriam's behalf and asked for her healing. In response to his call, God brought healing to Miriam's body and disciplined her only with seven days of isolation outside the Israelites' camp. Moses' act of forgiveness gave her a second chance with God!

God's Plan Needs You to Forgive

There are certain offenses that are especially difficult to put behind you. You may struggle with things that aren't difficult to others. For instance, you may feel that lying makes trust impossible, while a friend of yours may find it easy to forgive a lie if the intentions were sincere. You may find forgiving your husband's dabbling with pornography unthinkable, while another wife is able to forgive as long as there has been no adultery. You may find it exasperating that your wife spends money irresponsibly, while your friend is able to write off his wife's similar behavior as creative!

Some offenses, though, are almost universal in their ability to stifle reconciliation. An affair usually rips the soul of the offended spouse apart and builds a thick layer of resistance around the heart. The thought of being reconciled to your spouse who has been sexually involved with someone else is repulsive. It seems to be cemented in your heart that trust could never be rebuilt with this man who has disregarded his vows to you. Or you may be wondering if your wife could ever again be satisfied with you after having a fling with another man.

The insecurities you carry about yourself rush to the surface. You worry about your physical appearance and your ability to please your spouse. These fears are heightened by the fact that you are not interested in making love with the one who has violated your soul. So your insecurities are consistently chased to the forefront by your aversion to being with the one you want to be attractive to. The emotional turmoil of living with this inconsistency in your desires leaves you exhausted and frustrated. On the one hand, you want your marriage back. On the other hand, you can't stop the hurt that tempts you to hate the one you used to love.

But God often asks people to walk very difficult roads before he makes his grace known.

They married young, and people said they were the perfect couple. Their friends all thought they were getting along well, and his influence in the community was growing on a regular basis. Their reputation got bigger as they began having children. The birth of two sons and a daughter made them appear to be a happy family with a bright future.

But she was restless with family life. The daily routine was more than she was willing to endure, and so the affairs began. The thrill of unfaithfulness was more attractive to her than the responsibility of her marriage vows. This "modern" couple is Hosea and his wife Gomer, from the Old Testament.

Hosea was a prophet chosen by God to deliver a strategic message to the nation of Israel. The nation was prone to wander away from the worship of the true God and turn their affections to false idols. God compared this diversion in worship to an adulterous pattern in marriage. To assist the nation in understanding the pain and sense of betrayal associated with false worship, God asked Hosea to go through the painful process of being married to an adulterous wife.

> When the LORD began to speak through Hosea, the LORD said to him, "Go, take to yourself an adulterous wife and children of unfaithfulness, because the land is guilty of the vilest adultery in departing from the LORD." (Hos 1:2)

To illustrate the pain of betrayal and the power of forgiveness, God allowed Gomer to venture off into sexual relationships outside her marriage. After she was enmeshed in this lifestyle, God would then put obstacles in her way that would spoil her plans and leave her heart empty.

Therefore I will block her path with thornbushes;
    I will wall her in so that she cannot find her way.
She will chase after her lovers but not catch them;
    she will look for them but not find them.
Then she will say,
    "I will go back to my husband as at first,
    for then I was better off than now." (Hos 2:6-7)

In response Hosea would, in an amazing act of humility, open his heart and his arms and receive his estranged wife back. He would treat her with respect and affection but would require that she also treat him with respect and end the life of adultery. His own testimony is as follows:

> The LORD said to me, "Go, show your love to your wife again, though she is loved by another and is an adulteress. Love her as the LORD loves the Israelites, though they turn to other gods and love the sacred raisin cakes."
>
> Then I told her, "You are to live with me many days; you must not be a prostitute or be intimate with any man, and I will live with you." (Hos 3:1, 3)

Hosea trudged through a swamp of angry feelings over the betrayal by his wife. His heart must sometimes have been mired in disgust and rejection. But the plan of God was more important to Hosea than the breaking of his heart. God had a rugged road for Hosea to travel, and the only way to tune up for the journey was to master the art of forgiveness.

Preparing Your Lifestyle to Forgive

It is understandable to want to shield yourself from the devastating things that happen in this life. No one wants to be taken advantage of. It is especially understandable if you have been spun around by sexual, financial, physical or emotional turmoil. But the need to protect yourself is not a valid reason for keeping yourself tied in knots. You cannot free yourself from the devastation of the past by ensnaring yourself in the choking vines of bitterness. So how do you develop a plan that moves you beyond the fears of life?

Take charge! The life you are living today is the result of your response to the way you have been raised and the circumstances that have happened in your life. The way you live from today forward will be the result of the decisions you make. If you choose to continue the patterns of your past, then you will continue to have the same kind of life you have had. If you choose to learn new patterns of living, you will have a new kind of life. It is your choice.

The reason we have a hard time letting go of bitterness is often that the pain is caused by someone close. The wrong may have been done by a husband or a wife, a close family member or a close friend. These are relationships we are naturally motivated to maintain. We all have a sense of family in our hearts, and we all desire to be connected with these people. When these people violate the love that should be in families, we get put in a bind.

On the one hand, you hate what the person has done to you and wish you'd never see that person again. On the other hand, you have an emotional attachment to the person because you are both in the same family. You want this person's influence out of your life, but you want to have a strong dedicated family—a family that is connected and caring. You may think, *My family may not be the best, but at least they are there. They may have hurt me, but they take my phone calls. I don't like the way they treat me, but at least they pay attention to me.* The desire to be connected is one of the strongest drives of the human heart. Loneliness is a cruel companion. Loneliness was the one characteristic of creation that God said was not good.

If you have been hurt by your spouse or someone else close to you, you have the choice of how far-reaching the influence of that hurt will be. If you choose to focus on the hurt and dwell on your misfortune, you will continue to hurt. If you choose to focus on God's forgiveness and the possibilities of the future, you will grow and develop so that you can move beyond the pain as you discover a future of hope.

The reason the pain continues is that the influence of the one who has hurt you still runs strong. If you can get control of the direction of your life, then you will not be so susceptible to the waves of pain that accompany unchecked bitterness. Ask yourself the following questions: *What kind of reaction do I want to have to life? What area of life needs attention next? What reaction would I rather have to the circumstances of life than anger? depression? fear? If my best friend were facing this same situation, what advice would I give him or her?*

One of the tests of maturity is the ability to be in control of your emotional reactions. Children regularly have outbursts of emotions that take over and dictate their behavior. Mature adults, on the other hand, have the ability to choose the context for the release of their emotions. It is not that healthy adults shut down their emotions; it is just that they are able to wait for the appropriate time to let out emotions, and they are able to do so in appropriate ways. Without this important ability, you are caught in a life where things happen to you rather than a self-directed life.

Set boundaries. Your need to protect yourself will be better served by setting healthy boundaries[6] than by making wishes or building walls. Boundaries are limitations that you decide to set in order to keep your life healthy and maintain your self-respect. You maintain these boundaries because they fit your life and are good for yourself and other people.

Most people spend their lives making wishes or building walls. A wish requires the other party to respond favorably for the wish to come true. A wall may look like an impenetrable fortress but is in reality a beacon that points out a vulnerable area of life. Boundaries are set to express to others that you respect yourself and are not available to be taken advantage of. Let's look at the example of a woman who is constantly being criticized by her husband. He is abusive in his language and overbearing in conversation.

She may express a wish, saying, "It is not right for you talk to me like that." For this statement to have any effect, the husband must decide it is important to respect his wife and respond to her wish. It may sound as if the wife is making a firm statement of her conviction about how men should treat women, but in reality she is just making a wish. He can choose to respond however he wants to. He is still in control of her life.

She may build a wall, saying, "Don't talk to me like that!" On the surface, this appears to be a statement of strength that clearly points out the wife's conviction. But there is no action attached to this statement that empowers the wife. The only obvious truth is that the abusive statements of the husband are damaging to the wife. Therefore, if the husband feels compelled to hurt his wife, he knows exactly how and where to inflict pain.

Or she may set a boundary, saying, "You have one month to get help for this problem. If you do not get started in counseling, I will make an appointment for myself to get help in figuring out what I need to do to put an end to this." This statement is a call to action for the person causing the hurt, and, at the same time, it is a statement of action for the person setting the boundary. Without the action step, the statement is just a wish or a wall. With the action step, respect may be maintained, and change will come—whether the offender responds or not.

Build a healthy support network. Change is a traumatic experience, if it is real change. The kind of growth that leads you to new ways of thinking and living is just that—new! Picture the life you have been living as an island and the life you want to live as the mainland. Stretching between the two is a long bridge. The bridge represents the steps of growth that are necessary to fundamentally change the way you approach life.

When you start out on this journey of growth it is exciting. You can see where you have come from, and your heart is full of anticipation about your destination. And when you finally arrive at the mainland and get a solid grasp of healthy living, you are relieved to have arrived and thrilled with the new life. But when you are halfway there, it can be very disconcerting. You are at the height of the bridge; the wind is blowing and the fog is rolling in. You can't see land at either end. You know you are on the right track, but it feels so dark, so cold and so alone.

This is when you need to have people around you who will pray for you and cheer you on. You need friends who will reassure you that it is worth the struggle and the risk. You need fellow travelers who will remind you of the ineffectiveness of where you have come from. Without this support many people return to the old, unhealthy patterns because at least that miserable life is familiar. If you are seeking to master the process of forgiveness, look for a small group of people in your local church that cares for one another—and join in.

Focus on the Heart
Lord, your plan for my life assumes that I am stronger than I feel. Help me to have confidence that with your help my marriage can succeed, and help me to value your plan more than my own comfort.

A Step Toward Love
Begin meeting with two or three trusted friends on a weekly basis to pray for your marriages. Be honest about the needs in your marriage, though it is not necessary to share everything in detail. Ask your friends to share the concerns of their marriages as well. Pray for each other, asking God to strengthen each of your marriages.

Three

Getting Forgiveness in Focus

I*n chapter one we met Sean and Rita. They had managed to make quite a* mess out of their lives. Sean was in the selfish habit of burying himself in his work and then taking refuge in alcohol when things got tough. Rita in her loneliness turned to another man. It is no surprise that when Sean found out about the affair he ran to his first love, the bottle.

"When he first heard," recalls Rita, "he went ballistic! He went to a bar and got rip-roaring drunk and violent. My oldest son had to drag him out of a fight and take him home. I had left at that point because I was so afraid of Sean's hatred."

Sean and Rita had abandoned one another and hurt one another deeply. Mysteriously, they still longed to be connected. It was hard to admit, but they wanted the intimacy they had known early in their marriage to return. But if Sean and Rita were to come back to intimacy with one another, they would have to master forgiveness. The marred history of their relationship cannot be erased—it can only be forgiven. Their destructive reactions to one another's selfish decisions cannot be justified—they can only be forgiven.

For the couple who wants to recapture their love when it has been wounded, forgiveness is a must. The process is challenging, however, because there is much confusion about what forgiveness is and isn't. If we are going to get a handle on how to exercise forgiveness in our lives, we must have a clear understanding of just what we are dealing with. In this chapter, we will discuss some of the vital characteristics of forgiveness so we can avoid the common misconceptions.

Forgiveness Remembers

It is a common mistake to think that in order to forgive someone we have to forget the offense that has been done. Somehow we are expected to take emotionally significant negative events and put them out of our memories. We are not taught to do this with good memories because they help shape who we are and how we view life. In the same way, the negative events in life add to our development and mold our convictions. If you have had money stolen from you, you will most likely have strong convictions about robbery and financial integrity. If you have been abused, you probably have intense opinions about the need for children to be protected. If you have been raised in the home of an alcoholic, you will certainly not be neutral on the issue of the proper role of alcohol in life. If you have experienced the horror of rape, you probably hold strong values regarding the safety and protection of women.

The reason you have such strong opinions about these areas is that you *do* remember. The intensity you feel is based on your understanding of what others will experience. If you are on the path of trying to forget what happened, you run the risk of dulling your senses and establishing blind spots in your life. The key is to remember the event in a way that builds character and conviction in your life. You do not, however, want to remember in a way that causes you to reexperience the emotions associated with the event. If you go through the emotional trauma every time you remember the past, the past will be your master. You want to use the past to solidify your convictions, but you don't want the past to build fear that freezes you solid when you are faced with new challenges.

As Rita reminisced about the progression of her relationship with Sean, she began to formulate her plan. She did not ever want to go back to what they had before, because she remembered the pain. On the other hand, she didn't just want to run away from the relationship, because she remembered the good times. Her memories guided her actions.

"At that point, I had mixed feelings," Rita said with a remorseful tone. "I knew an affair was wrong. I knew it could destroy my marriage and my family, but it was the first time I could remember being happy—like my emotional needs were being met. I decided that I had to end the affair, but I also decided I had to draw the line for Sean. I demanded that he get help for his drinking and workaholism. I demanded that he love me like I deserved to be loved. I'd never felt like I deserved a great sex life or a wonderful relationship before, but now I knew I could have one and I wanted it with my husband.

"I gave an ultimatum: 'Sean, get some help or move out!'"

Sean remembers, "It was like a ticking clock around our house."

If Sean and Rita are to make changes that will lead them to a healthy relationship, they will have to be careful not to forget how they got in trouble. The memory of the pain will bring their motivation to the surface. The hope of what they could have will keep alive their desire to find a better way of interacting with each other. The shadow of their previous life will remind them of the mistakes they do not want to make again.

Forgiveness Promotes Excellence

In the relativistic world we live in, it seems that the highest goal of life is happiness. We are told that if we attain a satisfying level of happiness we have reached the top. We have a society that has replaced the idea that there are rights and wrongs with a frantic pursuit of personal peace and happiness. Something is considered *right* if it makes you happy and *wrong* if it takes your happiness away. As a result, many people mistakenly think forgiveness is simply a process of accepting other people's decisions. It is assumed that each of us is seeking our own happiness and that we have the right to do so.

But this plan is doomed to failure. It is not possible for everyone to be constantly happy in a world that is broken. Everybody has short-comings and all of us make mistakes. Those inconsistencies in human behavior hurt other people. You cannot say that another's actions are "OK" when that behavior is wrong. If somebody beats you, it is wrong. If someone steals from you, it is wrong. If another disregards your opinions and treats you with disrespect, it is wrong. We often sabotage our own healing because we won't face the moral reality of life. With no standard by which to evaluate life, forgiveness cannot be applied. Since forgiveness is the only recourse for many of the events of life, the offended individual is left in a powerless state where freedom from bit-terness is impossible. In order to empower forgiveness, there must be a desire to discover God's best in life.

Sean and Rita's breakthrough happened when they embraced the need for excellence. They had been living selfishly and carelessly when it came to their marriage. When they grew tired of the loneliness, they began looking for a new way to do things that was more focused on what was *right* than on what was *easy*.

"Day after day I waited for Sean to step up and be the husband I wanted, but day after day it was the same old thing," Rita stated with an obvious air of disappointment in her voice.

"That is, until that Sunday morning," Sean interjected. "I had grown up going to church, but I never really let it affect my everyday life. My granddad was a pastor, but my dad was a rebellious preacher's kid, and so my feelings about God were mixed. I kept going to church for our kids' sake, but I kept God at a distance.

"But that Sunday morning I came face to face with God—and myself. A man my age, a successful businessman like me, got up and told the story of his life. He drank. His wife felt abandoned. She had an affair. But then God intervened in his life, saved him from himself, and rescued his marriage and his family.

"It was like looking in the mirror. I knew I had to do the same thing as that stranger. I had to give up my way of running my life, give my life to God and let him have the CEO spot in my life. I knew I needed to do it right then or it would be too late. I was already feeling like all the things I loved and valued—my wife, the kids, our family—were slipping right through my fingers. It was now or never. That's why I stood in my living room and begged for forgiveness before all my family and friends. I had come to a dead end, and the only hope left was in seeking God's forgiveness and hoping that my wife and family would forgive me too."

Forgiveness Pursues Growth

The very nature of forgiveness drives us to look ahead. We are challenged to overcome the past with forgiveness so that we can move triumphantly into the future. In a relationship with Christ we are transformed from a life of foolishness, even sinfulness, to a life of productive service. In describing this process the apostle Paul says, "And that is what some of you were. But you were washed, you were sanctified, you were justified in the name of the Lord Jesus Christ and by the Spirit of our God" (1 Cor 6:11).

In a similar way, all relationships are called to continuous improvement. Many people recognize the necessity to grow beyond the intense feelings associated with the pain. But they avoid forgiving because replacing the hurt with a positive outlook and renewed hope in their relationship seems too hard.

Trying to ignore the irritations of life rather than grow beyond them will only put off the suffering. The reality is that life is a mixture of pleasure and pain. There are some great moments in life that create lifelong memories that sweeten our experience as human beings. But there are also some agonizing moments that threaten to drive us into a shell where we no longer risk the thrill of intimacy or the challenge of new opportunities.

None of us can run away from life for long. But all of us like to try at times because life is full of conflict. Sometimes life is just irritating.

Perhaps you married a woman who was so sweet at first that you thought you had found the well of compassion. But as time goes on you realize she is overwhelmed with making decisions because she feels everything so deeply. Or you married a man who made you feel secure by his strong decisiveness. As time goes on you feel run over by the quick, unemotional decisions he makes regarding issues you hold dear.

Instead of acknowledging your dissatisfaction and applying forgiveness when it is needed, you act as if you aren't hurt. Your spouse disappoints you, but you develop a stiff upper lip and act as if the ups and downs of life are not disruptive to you. You may even appear to have no needs. For years you play the part of the model citizen, dedicated spouse and committed church member. Then you suddenly explode and begin making drastic decisions about life. Instead of being a faithful spouse, you enter into an affair. This new, exciting partner seems more attractive than the constant responsibilities of family life. Or you may leave your hard-working pursuit of business for a new career where you can find yourself. Or your desire to finish your education may eclipse all concern about how the kids will be cared for. These decisions surprise everyone involved in your life because they appear out of character. You have appeared to be such a stable individual — but the reality is that you have stifled growth and allowed bitterness to slowly simmer under the mounting pile of dissatisfaction.

Rita and Sean came to realize that they needed to grow as individuals if they were going to ever have a successful relationship. Life had continued to grow, but they had stagnated. Life had presented bigger opportunities and more strenuous challenges, but they had remained developmentally small. Life was taking too much energy because they were trying to accomplish mature goals with adolescent skills.

"Sean had to forgive my affair. I had to forgive myself. Sean had to forgive himself, and we had to forgive each other. My folks divorced when I was a kid, and I didn't want that for my kids. Neither did Sean. We also didn't want to throw eighteen years of marriage down the drain. We had been a good team in the area of work and parenting, and we had a lot to lose if we left each other. I also knew that people tend to repeat cycles and if I didn't figure out what was wrong with me, I'd end up married to a man just like Sean all over again!"

Sean emphatically added, "Someone had to stand up and say, 'No, we're not going to lose this family. We're going to battle through this and get to a good place.' So that Sunday, I stood, but I also fell to my knees in surrender and prayed, 'God, do whatever it takes to set me straight.'"

"He was a broken man," Rita recalled, "and I needed to see that. Sean's asking for forgiveness was the first step in our healing. Later we went for counseling. There I learned about personalities. I grew to appreciate Sean. He was very different in temperament from me, and I used to take those differences personally. Like when I asked what he wanted to do on a date, he would say, 'I don't care.' I took that as indifference toward me, like he didn't care about me. But I found out that he really is just very content and honestly doesn't have a preference as to which movie or restaurant we should go to. Now I just plan the date, tell Sean, and we're both happy."

Their commitment to keep learning and growing as part of their forgiveness journey has kept them on the road to reconciliation.

Forgiveness Is Not Reconciliation

Although forgiveness and reconciliation are related to one another, they are not the same. There is a very distinct difference. Forgiveness is a process that takes place within the heart of an individual. It is an internal decision to release one's own heart from continued pain and manipulation. Reconciliation is a process that takes place between two parties. It is a decision to restore a broken relationship between them.

In our experience working with people, we often see people stall in their growth because they define forgiveness as reconciliation. Reconciliation is often frightening or repulsive because the offending individual has shown no remorse and has made no significant change. There is nothing to convince the offended individual that a new relationship would be any different than the previous one. Not knowing how to forgive without reconciling, the offended one falls into limbo and lives in the misery of thinking it is necessary to simply endure a relationship that has caused great pain.

The greatest distinction for our daily lives is the extent to which we apply forgiveness and reconciliation. *Forgiveness must be applied to every situation in our lives if we want to maintain our freedom to grow.* Bitterness is a process that will destroy the one who holds onto it. We must forgive, whether or not the other person wants to be forgiven. Then we can let go of our bitterness. *Reconciliation, on the other hand, is to be applied only to those who repent.* If the person who has caused you pain has not repented, apologized and committed to making changes in life, reconnecting to that individual will only cause further pain and hinder our own personal growth.

"There were days I was still really struggling to forgive Sean," Rita shared honestly. "I guess I never really understood how to forgive him—what it really meant. Then we went to a marriage conference our church hosted. The Farrels spoke about forgiveness and walked us through the steps of forgiveness. That's when I turned the corner emotionally. The hurt is coming off in layers, and now I know what to do with the hurt, how to handle it. I think God prepared me for this journey to forgiveness. Last winter I had pneumonia. I spent weeks in bed. For three to four hours a day I read my Bible. I felt stronger as an individual. By forgiving before trying to reconcile the situation, I was able to be happy and content, even though Sean was still drinking then."

Rita found a new stability in her life as she discovered the distinction between forgiveness and reconciliation. The heart of the Christian message points out this vital distinction. When Jesus died on the cross, he died for the sins of the whole world. His death and resurrection were sufficient to offer forgiveness to everyone on earth, without distinction. He does not, however, give salvation to everyone automatically. He requires that people repent from their own self-effort in trying to *earn* the right to be accepted into heaven and turn to him to receive his *gift* of forgiveness and eternal life. When an individual does so, God reconciles the relationship that should have been there all along. Jesus described eternal life as a relationship when he said,

"Now this is eternal life: that they may know you, the only true God, and Jesus Christ, whom you have sent" (Jn 17:3).

Forgiveness Must Come First

Forgiveness is the prerequisite that makes reconciliation possible. Without forgiveness, reconciliation cannot be realized because the resentment of bitterness interferes with the restoring of the relationship. It is possible to forgive all the hurts of our past without reconciling, but it is impossible to reconcile without first forgiving.

Esau was a man who had to learn this hard lesson of life. Esau was the firstborn son of a proud Jewish father, Isaac. He had the honor of inheriting the family birthright, which would make him the main decision-maker for the family and give him the bigger portion of the financial inheritance to empower those decisions. His future was secure, his confidence was high and his reputation was guaranteed. Then life got in the way of living.

Esau had been out working the herds and was starving. Jacob was at home cooking up some stew. The aroma of the fresh stew pierced Esau's hunger—and blew right past his sense of right and wrong.

> He said to Jacob, "Quick, let me have some of that red stew! I'm famished." . . .
> Jacob replied, "First sell me your birthright."
> "Look, I am about to die," Esau said. "What good is the birthright to me?"
> But Jacob said, "Swear to me first." So he swore an oath to him, selling his birthright to Jacob.
> Then Jacob gave Esau some bread and some lentil stew. He ate and drank, and then got up and left.
> So Esau despised his birthright. (Gen 25:30-34)

The story doesn't end there. At the end of Isaac's life, he sought to redeem his son Esau by giving him a blessing that would carry the authority of the patriarch. This blessing would give Esau some decision-making ability even though Jacob, holding the birthright, would still get the bigger portion of the inheritance.

But once again Jacob got the better of his brother. He stole the
blessing by impersonating Esau. He even used goatskins on his hands
and neck so his father, whose eyesight had failed, would think upon
touching him that he was the hairy Esau rather than the smooth-
skinned Jacob.

> Jacob said to his father, "I am Esau your firstborn. I have done as you
> told me. Please sit up and eat some of my game so that you may give me
> your blessing." . . . He did not recognize him, for his hands were hairy
> like those of his brother Esau, so he blessed him. (Gen 27:19, 23)

Having secured the blessing from his father, Jacob hightailed it
away before Esau got home and discovered his deceptive plan.

> After Isaac finished blessing him and Jacob had scarcely left his
> father's presence, his brother Esau came in from hunting. He too pre-
> pared some tasty food and brought it to his father. Then he said to him,
> "My father, sit up and eat some of my game, so that you may give me
> your blessing." (vv. 30-31)

But Esau was too late. Isaac had already given the privileges of the
patriarch to Jacob. Esau would be subservient to his younger brother
and wrestle with the bitter lot of having been manipulated.

> When Esau heard his father's words, he burst out with a loud and bit-
> ter cry and said to his father, "Bless me—me too, my father!"
>   But he said, "Your brother came deceitfully and took your blessing.
> . . . I have made him lord over you and have made all his relatives his
> servants, and I have sustained him with grain and new wine. So what
> can I possibly do for you, my son?" (vv. 34-37)

This last deceptive act of Jacob's was more than Esau could take. A
bolt of bitterness shot through his being. And with it came sorrow,
anger and a commitment to revenge.

> Esau held a grudge against Jacob because of the blessing his father had
> given him. He said to himself, "The days of mourning for my father are
> near; then I will kill my brother Jacob." (v. 41)

Esau and Jacob's connection as brothers made it inevitable that there would be a point in the future where their relationship would be tested. If Esau held onto this bitterness, reconciliation would be impossible. Without forgiveness, the attempt to reconcile would be a perfect opportunity for revenge. Amazingly, God got hold of Esau's heart and gave him the grace to forgive before the encounter. The two of them planned a meeting. They had lots of time to anticipate the encounter. Esau traveled to the reunion in peace, aware of the work of God's grace in his heart. Jacob, on the other hand, didn't know about the process that was being accomplished in Esau's heart, and so he approached him with fear and trembling. When the fateful day came,

> Jacob looked up and there was Esau, coming with his four hundred men; so he divided the children among Leah, Rachel and the two maidservants. He put the maidservants and their children in front, Leah and her children next, and Rachel and Joseph in the rear. He himself went on ahead and bowed down to the ground seven times as he approached his brother.
>
> But Esau ran to meet Jacob and embraced him; he threw his arms around his neck and kissed him. And they wept. (Gen 33:1-4)

Some people unwisely try to reconcile before they have been through the soul-searching process of forgiveness. If forgiveness has not been mastered but we reconcile anyway, we submit to tyranny. We say to others, "It is OK for you to mistreat me and exercise power over me. I will never make you responsible for your own actions." When we do this, we proclaim that we have no respect for ourselves or for the person we are reconciling with. When we allow ourselves to be mistreated, we become victims and we encourage others to be tyrants. As a result, the sensitive wound that has not been healed by forgiveness will be reopened by the mistreatment of the unrepentant individual. Forgiveness must precede reconciliation.

How does this apply when it comes to current, everyday relationships, like the interaction of a husband and wife? We cannot choose to just throw away a marriage because it has some problems. We cannot afford to break up families because the love between a husband and wife is being challenged.

Because marriage is a lifetime relationship, forgiveness and reconciliation take on a more specific nature. The couple may be doing well with interpersonal communication while not seeing eye to eye financially. They may be in sync with one another in their parenting priorities while having trouble feeling understood in their intimate interaction. Forgiveness is still needed for every conflict and is a prerequisite to resolving the issues.

Reconciliation, on the other hand, is applied in increments. If the finances of the home are not being handled well by one of the partners and a conflict results, forgiveness must be given. But in addition, the destructive principles of money management must be challenged and repentance in this area must be pursued. It may be that financial guidance from a qualified money manager will be appropriate, or maybe a mentor couple should be sought. The goal is that the money will be managed in a way that is comfortable for both partners. The change must be sought with tenderness but also with resolve.

If a couple is finding harmony as parents but struggling with their intimate conversation, pain will lurk around the edges. On the one hand, each of the spouses needs to keep forgiveness active in the heart, or else the possibility of finding fulfillment will become increasingly remote. On the other hand, neither of the spouses should settle for interaction that is not satisfying to either partner and that is interrupting their sexual unity. Actions to restore the intimacy of the relationship may include reading good books, attending marriage retreats or seminars and seeking out competent counseling. Often a troubled couple will find amazing help from another couple who is willing to be a mentor. The key is to (1) inundate your relationship with forgiveness, so that emotions don't interrupt the process of growth, and then (2) commit to working together on your relationship until it becomes more satisfying for you both.

Rita smiled as she said, "That Sunday morning last winter, Sean turned to me and said, 'How do you get that feeling?'

"'What feeling?'

"'You know—the happy, peaceful, close to God feeling. It seems so easy for you.'

"I explained that it was easy. Jesus was standing at the door of his life knocking, and if he'd just open the door and let God in, he'd feel it too. I took Sean by the shoulders that morning and said, 'I want to be married to you, more than anything else in life. I love you. I claim the victory. The victory over the hurt, the alcohol, over all the junk, is ours if you want it, Sean. We can have love again. God wants that. I want it. Do you want it? The choice is yours.'"

How about you? Do you want forgiveness? Do you want reconciliation?

The choice is yours!

Focus on the Heart
Oh, Lord, help me to see past the deceptions in my heart. I am so willing to accept substitutes for forgiveness, but I am tired of being held back. Help me to see that forgiveness is more powerful than anything I may try to put in its place.

A Step Toward Love
Have a conversation with your spouse about the substitutes for forgiveness to which you are most susceptible. Make this a positive experience. Plan a date where you can talk without distractions. Avoid any judgments that would interrupt freedom in sharing. For instance, do not ask, "How could you ever think that way?" or "I would never reach that conclusion." Instead, be grateful and encouraging.

Say to your spouse, "The misconception about forgiveness that holds me back most often is _____." Then fill in the blank with one of the following:

☐ thinking I have to forget what happened
☐ denying that what happened was really all that bad
☐ feeling I have to say that what happened was OK
☐ deciding I have to be stoic about what happened
☐ assuming I have to reconcile in order to forgive

Four

Bitterness
Barrier to Forgiveness

S*aul is an example of someone who got off to a great start—and then* allowed bitterness to dictate the emotional motivations of his life. His story is recorded in the book of 1 Samuel.

He was "an impressive young man without equal among the Israelites" (1 Sam 9:2), taller and stronger than his peers, and so he was the obvious choice to be king. But it didn't take long to reveal that the strongest motivations in Saul's life were negative. These basic emotions in his life created fertile ground in his heart for bitterness.

Saul had made the mistake of believing the rave reviews about himself. He had his important place in life, but he wanted more. Because he thought too highly of himself, he overstepped his authority.

His troops were in the midst of battle and were separated into two fronts. The soldiers who stayed with Saul "were quaking with fear" (1 Sam 13:7). Saul had been told to wait seven days for Samuel. When he arrived, Samuel would offer sacrifices and seek the Lord on behalf of Saul and the army to get their next directions. But Samuel was delayed.

And so Saul took things into his own hands. He called for the offering and burned it as a gift to the Lord. The problem was that Saul was
a king and not a priest, so he was therefore not allowed to offer sacrifices. But Saul talked himself into his own importance. He must have
thought, *I'm a king, and God has trusted me with the whole nation. Samuel is
late, and if I don't take action, my soldiers will scatter.* This thinking led Saul
to believe that he was "compelled to offer the burnt offering" (1 Sam
13:12).

When Samuel came, he responded bluntly: "You acted foolishly."

This was the beginning of the end for Saul. Samuel went on, "Now
your kingdom will not endure; the LORD has sought out a man after his
own heart and appointed him leader of his people, because you have
not kept the Lord's command" (1 Sam 13:14).

The realization that his kingdom was being taken away from him,
and the consequent realization that his son Jonathan would never
have the opportunity to rule, gripped Saul's heart deeply. A pattern of
bitterness began that day that consumed his whole life. As the bitterness evolved, Saul's emotional development eroded.

Forgiveness Is an Inside Job

In achieving forgiveness, it is vital that each of us understand the
internal nature of the forgiveness process. When bitterness takes
root in the heart, it becomes an internal drive that competes for
motivational control of life. It may manifest itself in outward behaviors, but it is primarily an inward struggle. The person who is harboring bitterness may appear to be struggling with anger, insecurity
or even some addictive behavior such as pornography. If the under-
lying struggle is bitterness, these behaviors are just symptoms of the
real problem. These are the defenses that are called out when the
alarms go off.

Bitterness Breeds Excuses

Saul was given the privilege and responsibility of leading the nation of
Israel. In this position, God gave him clear directions with regard to

military and political strategy. When God sent the army to fight the Amalekites, he told Saul, "Go and completely destroy those wicked people, the Amalekites; make war on them until you have wiped them out" (1 Sam 15:18). But Saul took things into his own hands and "spared Agag and the best of the sheep and cattle, the fat calves and lambs—everything that was good" (15:9).

Samuel confronted Saul with his lack of integrity. "What then is this bleating of sheep in my ears? What is this lowing of cattle that I hear? . . . Why did you not obey the LORD? Why did you pounce on the plunder and do evil in the eyes of the LORD?" (1 Sam 15:14, 19).

Instead of owning up to his mistake and seeking God's forgiveness and restoration, Saul made excuses for his behavior. "But I did obey the LORD," Saul said. "I went on the mission the LORD assigned me. I completely destroyed the Amalekites and brought back Agag their king. The soldiers took sheep and cattle from the plunder, the best of what was devoted to God, in order to sacrifice them to the LORD your God at Gilgal"(1 Sam 15:20-21). It is now not "my God" but "your God." Saul should be admitting responsibility. Instead he is making up excuses to justify his actions.

It is not uncommon for a marriage partner to resort to excuses when the commitment to serve one another seems too heavy. "I'd work harder if my family appreciated what I do." "I would be more cooperative if he was more sensitive." "I would forgive her, but I don't think she would repent." "God understands that I could never be happy in this marriage." Being married is a strenuous adventure, to be sure, but God help us if we think that excuses are more powerful than forgiveness.

Bitterness Breeds Insecurity

As Saul tried to deal with the downward turn in his kingdom without a repentant heart, he became an insecure leader. Rather than appealing to people based on the wisdom and integrity of his decisions, he became authoritarian in his demands.

In the midst of one of his battles, he foolishly "bound the people under an oath, saying, 'Cursed be any man who eats food before evening comes, before I have avenged myself on my enemies!'" (1 Sam 14:24). He now had an army fighting hard without any nourishment. Saul's son Jonathan didn't get news of the command not to eat, so while he was out in the woods, "he reached out the end of the staff that was in his hand and dipped it into the honeycomb. He raised his hand to his mouth, and his eyes brightened" (14:27). Saul was now in a mess. Should he admit that he had been wrong in giving a foolish order and humbly spare Jonathan's life, or should he stubbornly assert his authority and kill his son?

Amazingly, Saul chose that his word must stand, even though his word in this case was ridiculous.

Saul said to Jonathan, "Tell me what you have done."

So Jonathan told him, "I merely tasted a little honey with the end of my staff. And now must I die?" Saul said, "May God deal with me, be it ever so severely, if you do not die, Jonathan." But the men said to Saul, "Should Jonathan die—he who has brought about this great deliverance in Israel? Never! As surely as the LORD lives, not a hair of his head will fall to the ground, for he did this today with God's help." So the men rescued Jonathan, and he was not put to death. (1 Sam 14:43-45)

Saul's insecurity placed the people he most wanted to influence in a position where they had to resist him, thereby weakening his authority.

Like Saul, we get too attached to the harmful events of the past, and we use them to define who we are as people. The presence of Jesus in our lives challenges us to look at ourselves in a whole new light. We are not just talking about positive thinking in regard to ourselves. Instead we need to have a biblical view of our value as well as our shortcomings. The biblical approach is to realize that we all are created by God and treasured by him—seen as worth dying for!—but we are also flawed.

Jesus considers us so valuable that he has made us heirs to his riches and has put himself in us in the person of the Holy Spirit. But God is not blinded by our great value. He knows that we make mistakes and fall short, and he has placed in us the realization of our own failure. There is a war going on inside us. Part of us wants to do right, and part of us wants to do wrong. As a result, we have very successful days—and days where life gets in the way of living. The goal, in terms of our daily approach to life, is to be humbly confident: humble because we are aware of our shortcomings and our tendency to make mistakes; confident because the God of the universe has invested in us and has become a partner in life with us.

Those who carry wounds have a tendency to overemphasize one side of this truth. They may dwell on their shortcomings and focus on the areas of life that are not healthy. They reach the conclusion that they are deficient and have no significant place in life. This can lead to depression, overanalysis and poor decisions. If these people believed they were who God says they are, they would give themselves a better advantage in life and would make decisions that were healthier.

Others overemphasize their value in life. They lie to themselves about how good they are and how competent they are in their pursuits. They refuse to take an honest look at their shortcomings, and thereby they interrupt the growth process in their lives. As a result, they develop blind spots—areas of immaturity that are obvious to everybody except themselves. Conversations go awry, and others are blamed. Constructive criticism is ignored while the behavior is justified. Another's feelings are hurt, and that person is criticized for being too sensitive. The end result of all these actions is relationships that are strained and tense.

Bitterness Breeds Turmoil

When bitterness gains a foothold in the heart, turmoil is inevitable. The pain and the panic do laps in the inner person and look for places to lodge. Wherever the bitter seed implants itself, a malignant wound is produced. Saul's bitterness opened his heart to the influence of an evil spirit. "Now the Spirit of the LORD had departed from Saul, and an evil spirit from the LORD tormented him" (1 Sam 16:14).

The incessant turmoil in the heart of Saul manifested itself in rage and violence. First he lashed out against David, who was employed in his court as a musician and soldier. "An evil spirit from God came forcefully upon Saul. He was prophesying in his house, while David was playing the harp, as he usually did. Saul had a spear in his hand and he hurled it, saying to himself, 'I'll pin David to the wall.' But David eluded him twice" (1 Sam 18:10-11).

But the rage did not stop with David. Saul's son Jonathan had developed a close friendship with David and had helped David out more than once. Saul often got caught up agonizing over the fact that Jonathan would never be king. During one of these internal tirades, he turned his anger toward Jonathan because Jonathan did not seem to share his father's conviction about the importance of being king.

> Saul's anger flared up at Jonathan and he said to him, "You son of a perverse and rebellious woman! Don't I know that you have sided with the son of Jesse to your own shame and to the shame of the mother who bore you? As long as the son of Jesse lives on this earth, neither you nor your kingdom will be established. Now send and bring him to me, for he must die!"
>
> "Why should he be put to death? What has he done?" Jonathan asked his father. But Saul hurled his spear at him to kill him. (1 Sam 20:30-33)

Tragically, Saul's bitterness had now reached the point where he was willing to destroy the people he loved most on earth.

The dynamics of marriage are so intense that an otherwise loving couple can be turned into adversaries. Bitterness gives birth to criticism. Unchecked, criticism grows into assaults, abuse, public humiliation and constant antagonism. The real issue is that the bitter partner is in turmoil and is blaming it on the spouse.

Bitterness Breeds Hatred

Not even Saul's love for his daughter could stem the tide of bitterness in his life. "Michal was in love with David, and when they told Saul about it, he was pleased" (1 Sam 18:20). At first glance this seems to be progress, but we discover that Saul liked the idea because he believed he could use his daughter's love for David against David. Saul ordered his attendants to lobby David with the benefits of marrying Michal. He finally revealed his devious plan for the dowry when he said, "The king wants no other price for the bride than a hundred Philistine fore-skins, to take revenge on his enemies" (18:25). Saul figured that in the process of gathering the grisly dowry, David would be killed by the Philistines. He hated David to the point that he would use the love of his daughter to end David's life.

At first, it appears this was only Saul's problem, but later we see Michal amazingly developing the same hatred for David that Saul pos-sessed. Ironically, the event that brought this hatred to the surface was a worship celebration. The ark of the covenant had been in safe keep-ing at the home of a fellow Israelite during the times of conflict between David and Saul. In response, God had honored this man's family with peace and caused his business ventures to flourish. When David (now king of Israel) was told, he went to the man's house and moved the ark to his own city so that it could be with the king.

As the ark was brought into the city, "David, wearing a linen ephod, danced before the LORD with all his might, while he and the entire house of Israel brought up the ark of the LORD with shouts and the sound of trumpets" (2 Sam 6:14-15). David's passion for the Lord was obvious in his dancing. But instead of rejoicing with him, Michal despised him in her heart and openly criticized him out of embarrass-ment for her own reputation (vv. 16, 20). What started out as political enmity between two leaders extended into a deep-seated hatred between two lovers.

Bitterness Breeds Fear

Bitterness is a relentless disease that will stop growing only if it is removed by the surgery of forgiveness. The next symptom to develop in the life of Saul was fear.

Fear of failure. Goliath's challenge, "Give me a man and let us fight together" (1 Sam 17:10), brought to the surface Saul's nagging fear of failure. Rather than viewing this challenge as an opportunity for God

to show how powerful he was, Saul turned his eyes inward. "On hearing the Philistine's words, Saul and all the Israelites were dismayed
and terrified" (v. 11).

Fear of other people's success. David looked at the giant Philistine
through the eyes of faith and saw a much different picture than Saul
did. He saw a challenge that was not a big thing for God to deal with.
With courage in his heart, David faced the giant and won.

When the men were returning home after David had killed the Philistine, the women came out from all the towns of Israel to meet King Saul
with singing and dancing, with joyful songs and with tambourines and
lutes. As they danced, they sang:

"Saul has slain his thousands,
and David his tens of thousands."

Saul was very angry; this refrain galled him. "They have credited
David with tens of thousands," he thought, "but me with only thou-
sands. What more can he get but the kingdom?" And from that time on
Saul kept a jealous eye on David. (1 Sam 18:6-9)

This struggle continued to escalate throughout Saul's life. As
David's success grew, Saul's fear grew.

In everything he did he had great success, because the LORD was with
him. When Saul saw how successful he was, he was afraid of him. (vv.
14-15)

Fear of abandonment. The bitterness in Saul's heart eventually
gave birth to paranoia. He started believing there was a conspiracy
against him and that everyone in his kingdom would eventually
mutiny against him. The evidence indicated that Jonathan, David
and all the subjects still respected Saul and would remain faithful.
But bitterness had a more consistent voice. Saul revealed the fear in
his heart when he said,

Listen, men of Benjamin! Will the son of Jesse give all of you fields and
vineyards? Will he make all of you commanders of thousands and commanders of hundreds? Is that why you have all conspired against me?

No one tells me when my son makes a covenant with the son of Jesse.
None of you is concerned about me or tells me that my son has incited
my servant to lie in wait for me, as he does today. (1 Sam 22:7-8).

David was not lying in wait for him. In truth, David had chances to
kill King Saul and refused. But fear had taken over.

When fear takes over in a marriage, intimacy is impossible because
trust is gone. "There is no fear in love. But perfect love drives out fear,
because fear has to do with punishment. The one who fears is not made
perfect in love" (1 Jn 4:18). Fear is the unmistakable symptom that
love has been overpowered. In this environment a couple may be able
to coexist, but the only way they can get any form of intimacy back is
through courageous forgiveness.

Bitterness Breeds Contempt

Eventually bitterness excludes from its presence everything that is
decent. Saul's hatred for David reached so far into his heart that he
even held the priests of the living God in contempt. There was a group
of priests in the town of Nob who helped David and his followers
while they were in exile, running for their lives away from Saul. Saul
sternly said to these priests, "Why have you conspired against me, you
and the son of Jesse, giving him bread and a sword and inquiring of
God for him, so that he has rebelled against me and lies in wait for me,
as he does today?" (1 Sam 22:13).

When the priests readily admitted they had helped David, Saul
turned to his soldiers and said, "Turn and kill the priests of the LORD,
because they too have sided with David. They knew he was fleeing, yet
they did not tell me" (v. 17). Everyone in the town of Nob was slaugh-
tered that day because of Saul's paranoia—all because of bitterness.

In the same kind of overreaction, a bitterly contemptuous husband
may replace the love of his wife with pornography, crude behavior and
unhealthy associations. A bitter wife who has lost self-respect may
shun her husband—or replace him with a more "ideal" relationship.
Because these decisions are based on a warped sense of morality, the
end results will be tragic.

Saul was a passionate man with high ambitions in life. At one time he deeply loved his God, his country and his family. His life became a tragedy because he was committed to harboring bitterness. In contrast, David dedicated himself to mastering forgiveness even though he made some horrendous mistakes. As a result, "The war between the house of Saul and the house of David lasted a long time. David grew stronger and stronger, while the house of Saul grew weaker and weaker" (2 Sam 3:1).

The Strategic Question

How do you know if your struggle is just a relationship problem or if it is a matter of forgiveness? This is one of the strategic questions of life. In order to decide whether you need further relational training or a cleansing of your heart, ask yourself the following questions.

1. When my spouse agrees to work on a specific struggle in our relationship, do I feel better or worse? Diane was convinced that Dan didn't value her very much. She felt he was impossible to please and placed unrealistic demands on her. In addition, she often reminded him, "You just don't understand me. You make me feel just as useless as my mom did." Dan agreed to work on their relationship and committed to visiting a counselor with Diane.

The training was exciting at first, as they learned new ways to listen to each other. But as time went on, Diane found herself increasingly frustrated with Dan. Rather than appreciating the fact that her husband was growing and applying himself to trying to improve his communication skill, she was growing increasingly disgruntled with Dan's lack of understanding. It seemed the more he grew, the higher her expectations grew. The more he communicated, the more she accused him of being an uncaring individual. He was trying to reach her, while she was saying that he didn't "get it." If your spouse is making progress but you cannot accept that the growth is genuine, you may be struggling with a subtle form of bitterness.

2. Are there trigger events in our relationship? A trigger event takes place when you have an emotional overreaction to a situation. Your spouse asks you a simple question, and you explode in anger. Your child asks you a question, and you immediately feel overwhelmed by the responsibility of life. You have an awkward moment in your romantic life, and you feel totally rejected and worthless. Trigger reactions are sirens that warn you that bitterness has invaded your heart.

3. Do I feel unworthy of an intimate relationship? People who harbor bitterness will often feel that the efforts of their spouses are a waste of time. They can see their spouses exercising sincere efforts to break through to them, but they are convinced the love is simply an obligation on the part of the other.

You only love me because you have to. You only married me because you really didn't know me. If you had known me fully back then, you would have said no to spending your whole life with me. These were thoughts that did laps in Jenny's mind. Her relationship with Jared was better than most of the marriages she saw, but she could never believe that Jared was sincere. She consistently felt like a burden to him.

4. When I experience external success, do I feel better or worse? If you struggle with bitterness, you will find little joy in the successes of your life. A nagging sense of unworthiness haunts you. When things are getting better in your marriage, in your family or in your work habits, you become increasingly depressed or frustrated. You press on to find the fulfillment you thought you were looking for—only to discover you are nowhere near being happy. The improvements that should have been satisfying only expose more pain. Each unfulfilling achievement is accompanied with thoughts such as *I thought this would be enough, but obviously I must do a little better. If I lose a little more weight, my husband will be happy with me. If I get a little more organized, my wife will be proud of me.*

Each of these self-defeating comments is like an arrow pointing toward an insecure heart. The bitterness may be there because of something your spouse has done, or it may have been placed there in your past. Either way, it has the same devastating impact on your marriage. It is as if the shortcomings of your life distract you from seeing the core of bitterness that exists. If you can be upset about the lack of intimacy in your marriage, you don't have to look deeper in your heart.

If your career requires intense focus, you don't have to focus on the challenge of being a good spouse. As other areas of life improve, the core of bitterness becomes more obvious.

Terry had spent the last fifteen years building a successful life. He married a woman who was industrious and dedicated to the family. He pursued a highly technical career that was on the cutting edge of progress. He had a nice home, two relatively new cars and an adequate savings account. As the strain of life eased with his success, a gnawing sense of unhappiness gripped him. It started as a general feeling that something was missing from his life. He would go to work and be bored with what used to be challenging. He would come home and get frustrated with the casual attitude his family had toward the things he had worked so hard to obtain.

Terry then found a new love in writing. He had buried this skill as a child because his parents made it clear they did not approve of his pursuing a craft that would not make large amounts of money. Instead he was encouraged to pursue engineering and analytical skills and criticized for his artistic interests. He committed himself to technical training, not realizing that his decision was cementing a bitterness into his heart that would eventually interrupt his life. Now he began to write poetry, short stories and in-depth journal articles. It became the one pursuit in life that brought him any satisfaction.

As he journaled consistently, it became clear to him that he had been allowing people to set up unrealistic expectations for him. His wife regularly committed him to social obligations and home projects without his consent. The family spent money without any consideration for the budget that he was responsible to balance. At work he had the reputation for always being willing to take on extra responsibilities. This habit had started in the home he grew up in, was reinforced during his school years and had finally become solidified as his way of life.

Over the years, he had distracted himself from the pain by staying busy and achieving a level of success that made it seem as if he was living up to the expectations that hovered around him. At the core of

Terry's struggle was his animosity toward all these expectations and the individuals who had imposed them. The success hadn't worked. The more he advanced in his career, the more he was unhappy with his marriage. He kept thinking that if his wife changed he would feel better, but the expectations he put on her weren't satisfying either. Finally he reluctantly admitted that the problem must be within himself. That was Terry's first step toward finding help and health.

Focus on the Heart

God of grace, help me to want the freedom of forgiveness more than the comfort of clinging to bitterness. I am weary of the draining influence of holding on to the pain others have inflicted on me. Lord, I want your best for my life.

A Step Toward Love

Honestly ask yourself the strategic questions from this chapter.

☐ When my spouse agrees to work on a specific struggle in our relationship, do I feel better or worse?

☐ Are there trigger events in my relationship?

☐ Do I feel unworthy of an intimate relationship?

☐ When I experience external success, do I feel better or worse?

If you determine that the struggles in your marriage are primarily caused by bitterness in your heart, write a letter to your spouse saying you are sorry for taking out your bitterness on the marriage relationship. Then ask your spouse to pray for you as you work to replace the bitterness with a lifestyle of forgiveness.

Five

Choosing to Forgive

I*t's a girl!*"

Jan and Marc had been divorced for years but had come together to witness the birth of their first granddaughter.

"We all stood and cheered," remembers Jan. "No amount of awkwardness was going to rob from the joy of this moment."

"Jan was handling it well," lamented Marc, "but I wasn't. In that moment, the consequences of my affair years ago became all too clear to me. I had given up a loving wife, great kids and my self-respect for an affair with a woman at work who wanted to climb the financial and social ladder. I had simply been one rung on the ladder for her. I now wanted what I saw in my daughter's life—a home, a family, a legacy to leave my children—but I had none of it, and it stung."

Jan's decision years ago to forgive Marc had made this celebration possible. The birth of their granddaughter opened up Marc's heart to consider his own need for forgiveness.

"Jan had been a gem," Marc reminisced. "She never ran me down.

She never made snide remarks. She had even encouraged the children to keep up a relationship with me, when what they wanted to do was harbor bitterness and anger—justifiably so—against me. I looked over at Jan that night, and she looked tired. She had been at my daughter's side for weeks helping her."

"'Do you want to go get something to eat?' I asked her."

"Sure."

"Over dinner we talked of her plans to move to Colorado to start a new business a few weeks later. She seemed to have such hope and joy. Before she left, I made plans to help her pack up her things.

When I arrived to help, I noticed her arm in a brace. She'd had surgery. She could barely move it.

"'How are you going to drive?' I said. 'You can't drive.'"

"I guess you'll just have to drive me, then," Jan said with a smile.

"I agreed to do it. And it surprised me," Marc said tentatively. "I wasn't even anxious about being locked in a car for hours with my ex-wife. I hadn't spent any time with her for months, no, years. Now I was going to drive her halfway across the country, and it seemed like the right thing to do. I called work and told them I wouldn't be in for a few days. I couldn't believe myself. I never missed work for anything.

"For the two days in the car I felt appreciated, accepted, cared for, and like I'd found a long-lost friend. *How can she treat me like this?* I was a scum—I had an affair. *I was wrong, so very wrong.* She'd lost so much because of my wrong decisions, yet I felt no judgment from her.

"When we landed in Santa Fe, New Mexico, we spent the day shopping, eating, walking and talking—really talking. We talked about what we'd done right. We'd raised great kids. We had wonderful family memories from over twenty-five years together. We had a wonderful new little grandbaby. Jan put me on the plane and I went back to California. I tried to go back to work but I couldn't get Jan out of my mind. I called her daily with reports about our new granddaughter and to see how she was faring in her new job.

"A few months later, words came out of my mouth that surprised even me.

"'Jan, I think I should be telling you I love you. I can't fathom life without you. I think we should be together.'

"Jan said, 'OK.'

"'How can you say "OK?" I've hurt you so bad. I was terrible!'

"Six months later Jan was in my arms again," Marc remembers joyfully. "This time to stay. We renewed our vows. And four years and several grandchildren later, we are together, laughing, joking and building a new legacy to pass on to our grandchildren—the legacy of God's forgiveness."

"Marc, I worked through that years ago," Jan reassured him. "About two years after our divorce, I began to analyze my feelings. The first few years were such a blur of change that it took that long before I was ready to look at my feelings. I pictured you as my best friend, Marc, and that something bad had happened to you. Life had blindsided you, and you were a casualty of the world we live in. But for God's grace, it could have been me who had made the choice. I decided the most important thing was to realize that we are all human and it could have happened to me. You weren't out to hurt me. You weren't out to hurt anyone. I just went back to the place I first fell in love with you and let those feelings wash over me. I fluffed up the feelings of when we were first together, and I forgave you."

The Power of Forgiveness

Forgiveness is the treatment that heals relationships. Forgiveness is, first of all, at the heart of salvation. When God looked upon mankind to determine what our greatest need was, he concluded that forgiveness for our shortcomings and failures was the issue that demanded his greatest attention (Rom 5:8). He then gave his greatest gift, his only Son, to pay the penalty for our incompetence. As we receive the forgiveness God offers, we also receive eternal life and an unbreakable relationship with him.

When a friendship is threatened by behavior that is harmful or inconsiderate, forgiveness is the one issue that can give that friendship a fresh start. When a married couple offends each other and finds their relationship deteriorating because of the conflicts of life, forgiveness is the one device available to them that can lay the foundation for a new system of love and support.

Forgiveness is the greatest force for healing in relationships, because bitterness is the most destructive force on earth. Bitterness will redefine the ones you love and turn them into twisted and deformed gargoyles. Bitterness will blind your eyes to the positive qualities that your mate possesses. Bitterness will attempt to replace all other influences and become the master of your emotional life. Once bitterness takes over, it will relentlessly dull your senses and destroy your life.

Forgiveness, on the other hand, is an act of the will that brings freedom to the one who exercises it. At its core, *forgiveness is a decision you make to not allow anyone else to control your life.* Every area of bitterness that develops in your heart is a place from which the one who offended you can control your reactions to the events of life. If you see someone who reminds you of the one who hurt you, you react with anger or fear. When you are criticized, you feel insecure and question your ability to accomplish anything worthwhile. You are so afraid of disappointing other people that you avoid new opportunities even when you know they would be fulfilling. These are all examples of how past hurts take control over emotional responses to life. True forgiveness includes a decision on your part that the actions of another will not ruin your life. It is an agreement you make with God to leave in his hands the judgment for wrong done against you.

Joseph is probably the greatest example in the Bible of someone who mastered the process of forgiveness. His started out as a charmed life. His dad loved him "more than any of his other sons" (Gen 37:3). He was given special privileges alongside his dad rather than having to do manual labor with his brothers. His wardrobe was first-class, and opportunities for learning and growing were abundant.

All these privileges caused his brothers to be intensely jealous of him. The jealousy brewed into bitterness, and bitterness took action. When Joseph's father sent him to his brothers in the pasture with sup-

plies, the brothers sold him into slavery. At the slave-owner's final car-
avan stop, Joseph found himself in Egypt (Gen 37:23-28).

Rather than wallow in depression and bitterness, Joseph pulled
himself together and proved his worth to his master, Potiphar. He was
successful enough that he was put in charge of the estate and became
the CEO of Potiphar's enterprises.

He was attractive to women, and Potiphar's wife decided that he
would be the catch that would fulfill her hunt. Embittered by Joseph's
refusal of her advances, she falsely accused him of rape and had him
arrested. Joseph spent the next few years of his life in jail (Gen 39:11-
20).

Because Joseph chose to forgive relentlessly, his heart stayed clear
and his energy level stayed high. Even in prison he succeeded. The
quality of his character was so obvious that the jailer used him to help
manage the prison. One of his God-given skills was the ability to interpret dreams. This skill was used by a couple of men in the jail, and
word finally got to Pharaoh. Pharaoh had a dream that no one else
could interpret for him, so Joseph was called for. Joseph's interpretation was so insightful that he was not only released from prison but put
in charge of the whole country. He managed the seven years of good
harvests followed by seven years of famine that Pharoah's dream had
predicted.

After Joseph built up the reserves in Egypt, the famine drove his
brothers to come to him for relief. Time froze as Joseph recognized his
brothers. He had the authority to do whatever he wanted with them.
He could punish them for their betrayal, frighten them with his position or reconcile the relationship.

> Then Joseph could no longer control himself before all his attendants,
> and he cried out, "Have everyone leave my presence!" So there was no
> one with Joseph when he made himself known to his brothers. And he
> wept so loudly that the Egyptians heard him, and Pharaoh's household
> heard about it.
> Joseph said to his brothers, "I am Joseph! Is my father still living?"

But his brothers were not able to answer him, because they were terrified at his presence. Then Joseph said to his brothers, "Come close to me." When they had done so, he said, "I am your brother Joseph, the one you sold into Egypt! And now, do not be distressed and do not be angry with yourselves for selling me here, because it was to save lives that God sent me ahead of you. For two years now there has been famine in the land, and for the next five years there will not be plowing and reaping. But God sent me ahead of you to preserve for you a remnant on earth and to save your lives by a great deliverance.

"So then, it was not you who sent me here, but God. He made me father to Pharaoh, lord of his entire household and ruler of all Egypt. Now hurry back to my father and say to him, 'This is what your son Joseph says: God has made me lord of all Egypt. Come down to me; don't delay. You shall live in the region of Goshen and be near me— you, your children and grandchildren, your flocks and herds, and all you have. I will provide for you there, because five years of famine are still to come. Otherwise you and your household and all who belong to you will become destitute.' (Gen 45:1-11)

"You intended to harm me, but God intended it for good to accomplish what is now being done, the saving of many lives." (Gen 50:20)

The Six Statements of Forgiveness

In our ministry, we have tried to pattern forgiveness after Christ and his ultimate act of forgiveness on the cross. To create "handles" by which we can grasp forgiveness in a practical way, we have come up with the following six statements.

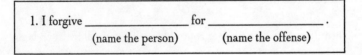

1. I forgive _____ for _____ .
      (name the person)   (name the offense)

"I am your brother Joseph, the one you sold into Egypt!" Notice that Joseph identifies not only the ones who did the deed but exactly what the deed was. It is important to specifically name the offense. Vague-

ness in dealing with forgiveness only leads to doubts about whether forgiveness has truly been achieved. We get hurt by individual acts done by others, or we ache under the pressure of specific characteristics in others' lives. We must identify these acts and characteristics specifically if we are to get out from under their influence. If you resort to general statements such as, "I forgive Susie for all the things she has done to me," or "I forgive John for being a jerk," you will never dislodge the anger that is attached to the specifics that have happened in your life. The healing of forgiveness will lie buried under layers of generalities.

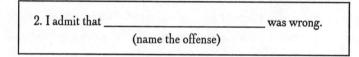

2. I admit that _____ was wrong.
(name the offense)

"You intended to harm me." Joseph was fully aware of the wrongness of his brothers' actions. This realization enabled him to see that his troubles were not his fault. He could therefore focus himself on finding God's blessing in the midst of a bad situation.

The greatest example of forgiveness in the world is the forgiveness Jesus Christ has offered us. He has granted to each of us who will trust him freedom from guilt. This is indeed good news! But the good news starts with a very tough reality. "All have sinned and fall short of the glory of God" (Rom 3:23). Paul increases the seriousness of forgiveness when he writes, "The wages of sin is death" (6:23). Paul understands forgiveness to be a life-and-death issue, which begins with the honest confession of something done wrong. In our politically correct world, we often feel uncomfortable saying something is wrong. We may feel we are being critical or judgmental. But if nothing wrong was done, there is nothing to forgive. And if the goal is forgiveness with the hope of reconciliation, you aren't being a critic or a judge—you are taking courageous steps of love.

This step is especially important for building up the confidence of the one who has been wronged. If reconciliation is in the future, the offended partner and the offending one must be able to approach the renewal of the relationship on equal footing. There must be the sense that both partners bring equal power and bargaining positions to the table when reconciliation is discussed. If you are afraid to admit that your partner's actions were wrong, then you put yourself in a subordinate position. In essence you are saying that all conflict is just a battle of opinions: since you were hurt by the decision of the other, you must have the weaker opinion. In order to truly rebuild a relationship, you must approach each other as equals.

If reconciliation is not in the future, say in the case of abuse, then the offended person must be free to set up firm convictions about the circumstances that brought about the offense. The intense emotions of bitter relationships create a strange curiosity. The offended individual is often drawn back to the harmful relationship in order to try to understand what caused the abuse. You may be wondering what it is about you that caused this person to hurt you, and you think that if you spend some time together you might discover it. Or you may be wondering what it is about that person that led to you be taken advantage of. If you do not have strong convictions about the wrongdoing, you run the risk of getting drawn back into the behaviors that caused your pain in the first place.

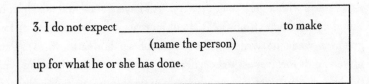

3. I do not expect _____ to make
         (name the person)
up for what he or she has done.

"Do not be distressed and do not be angry with yourselves for selling me here, because it was to save lives that God sent me ahead of you." Too often we expect the person who hurt us to come back, apologize profusely and beg our forgiveness. This rarely happens, and when it does it starts the pain all over again. Joseph had to wait years to have any communica-

tion with his family. If he had been waiting to forgive until he received an apology from his brothers, he would have wasted the most productive years of his life. Too many of us put our personal growth on hold as we sit around waiting for the phone to ring. Even if the person comes and asks our forgiveness—and maybe offers a gift to try to make up for the offense—nothing, absolutely nothing, can ever undo what was done. Once an offense is committed, it cannot be uncommitted. What is needed is to let the person off the hook.

By letting him or her off the hook, you are not saying that the offense is any less wrong. Nor are you saying that there will be no consequences. By not expecting the person to make up for the offense, you are turning the right to revenge over to God. You are trusting that God will hold the person accountable for his or her actions. You give up the right to be the hangman.

The real tragedy in not forgiving shows up here. If you refuse to let the one who hurt you off the hook, you insure that your life will be repeatedly affected by this same person. Too many people withhold forgiveness until they receive an apology. As you are waiting, the one who hurt you may be going on with life without a thought about how you are doing. As you repeatedly feel the pain, you pay the price for your victimization over and over again. There is no need to allow the one who hurt you to have further victory over your life. Don't wait! Get that person out of the loop of your emotional life.

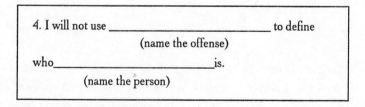

4. I will not use _____ to define
                        (name the offense)
who_____is.
        (name the person)

"So then, it was not you who sent me here, but God." Rather than referring to his brothers as the guys who put him through the wringer and ruined his life, he saw them as instruments in God's hands. They tried

to destroy him, but God turned their ruthless actions into a redeeming influence for Joseph, his family and the entire nation of Israel.

When you define people by the negative impact they have had on your life, you make them bigger than life. Too often we will define an adversary as *the person who ruined my life* or *the one who made me miserable.* As you do this, you give that person the ability to determine the state of your life. You choose to be miserable or to live with a dark shadow over you because of the actions of a person who has been unfair to you. You are chained to this person emotionally while you desperately need to be free.

When it comes to forgiving *yourself* of the things you have done, this step is vital. When you define yourself by the things you have done wrong, you encourage a process of decay. It has been well established that we live out what we think about ourselves. If you think you deserve an unhealthy life, you will live out an unhealthy life. If you think you deserve to be punished, you will live out a self-destructive life. If you think you are a failure, you will avoid the path of success. If, on the other hand, you define yourself as the object of God's forgiving grace and an adopted child who is in line for God's favor, you will pursue healthy avenues of growth and development.

---

5. I will not manipulate _____

(name the person)

with this offense.

"Come down to me; don't delay. You shall live in the region of Goshen and be near me —you, your children and grandchildren, your flocks and herds, and all you have. I will provide for you there." Can you imagine the power Joseph could have exercised over his brothers if he was inclined to manipulation? He could have made them his slaves. He could have punished them incessantly. He could have put them on a roller-coaster ride of failure by stealing whatever they produced. But Joseph didn't want to

ruin them—or himself!

Manipulation is an attempt to emotionally blackmail another person. It is an attempt to protect yourself from the influence another person has had on you. There is something in the human spirit that believes we can control another's influence through manipulation. The tragedy is that every act of manipulation confirms that the one who hurt you still has control of your life. Your very approach to life shows that your are still afraid of what this person might do to you, so you try to get to others before they get to you. You run in an endless circle of self-protection, never enjoying the freedom of truly living.

Jesus does not constantly bring up our past sins to force us to do his will. Rather, he calls us to walk with him as new creatures who have been set free from the past and our mistakes (see 1 Cor 5:17; Gal 2:20). We are encouraged to live as saints rather than as recovering sinners (Gal 5:1; 13:1; 1 Pet 2:16). This does not mean God ignores the influence of our past. He has committed himself to helping us grow through our past and reach up to a whole new life. We would be wise to look forward to the life ahead of us rather than constantly trying to overcome what is behind us.

---

6. I will not allow _____

                            (name the offense)

to stop my personal growth.

"It was not you who sent me here, but God. He made me father to Pharaoh, lord of his entire household and ruler of all Egypt." Joseph did not spend the difficult years of his life in frustration and despair. Rather he used those years to develop the character and leadership ability that God would eventually use to stage Joseph's finest hour.

Too often we allow the sinful offenses of others to dictate the course of our life. It is almost as if we think we are punishing the ones who hurt us as we refuse to pull our lives together. Or we are emotionally committed to keeping things the way they have historically been in our families. If our parents were bitter, then we are bitter. If the people in our families of origin were prone to depression, then we may be prone to depression. This applies to everything from alcoholism to anger to low self-esteem.

The influence of the hurts of the past can have a drastic impact on the decisions of everyday life. The only way to navigate around these inconsistencies is to deliberately choose the direction that your life will take. You must choose to live a way that is new—a way that is different from the past. You must grow beyond the influence of the hurt in your life. If you choose to wallow in the hurts of your life, you will find yourself repeating the same pain. The circumstances keep changing, but the pattern remains constant.

Clearing Your Conscience

If there are situations in your life to which you need to apply forgiveness, try following these steps:

1. Pray. Ask God to reveal to your mind anyone you need to forgive and the specific offenses involved. It is far too easy to overanalyze our lives and make mistakes in our conclusions when strong emotions are involved. We may come up with situations that didn't actually happen, we may exaggerate the severity of the offense or we may diminish the seriousness of a significant event. It is wise to ask for help from the One who holds abundant wisdom.

Steven found that his relationship with Sherry kept being interrupted by strong emotions that would suddenly spring on him and cause him to shut down emotionally. Sherry found herself becoming increasingly frustrated with Steven because just about the time their conversations would get close to the heart of their struggles with one another, he would go numb and quit talking. Steven knew there was something going on inside of him that was beyond his relationship with Sherry, but he couldn't seem to get at it. He began to pray and ask God to show him what was going on.

As he did, issues with his mom began to surface. Steven had grown up in a home where Mom was dominant and demanding. She often pointed out Steven's shortcomings in an attempt to make him more responsible. Instead of seeing her motivation, Steven believed that he could never do enough to please his mom. He spent most of his life trying to get Mom to say, "Well done, Steven. This is good enough." When Steven married Sherry, he assumed that Sherry would be different. But Sherry had needs and was not afraid to express them. Each time she would make her needs known, Steven would assume she was unhappy with him, and the old messages of inadequacy would kick into gear. Steven finally began to understand that much of the trouble between him and Sherry was really a struggle between him and his mom.

2. *Make a list.* As situations you need to forgive come to mind, write them down. You don't need to go into detail with what happened, but include enough of a description to clearly identify the specific offenses. As you deal with each of the offenses, you will be able to cross them off the list and have a written record of the progress you have made in releasing yourself.

Steven wrote down the issues he had with his mom and was surprised at how long the list was. She was critical of his pursuits. She withheld encouragement when he did well. She gave long lectures when she was mad. She threw things at him in anger; once she had even thrown hot coffee on him when he disagreed with her. She wanted him to be an actor; he wanted to be an athlete. So when he chose to play sports in high school, she refused to come to his games. He made a list of each of these and was amazed at how good it felt to put a line through the ones he was able to forgive at the first sitting.

3. *Take each situation on your list through the six statements of forgiveness.* As you attempt to sincerely voice each statement with the items on your list, you will find that the offenses you are ready to forgive will flow relatively smoothly. You will feel a sense of freedom and confidence in your heart as you release the animosity that is directed toward each specific event. On the other hand, you will stall on the offenses you are not ready to forgive. You will feel resistance in your heart, and

it will be obvious that you aren't really sincere. In this way, the six statements serve as a test for your heart to see if you have accomplished forgiveness or if you are just hovering around the edge looking in.

Steven started with his mom's lack of attendance at his sporting events because it was the situation that had the least pain associated with it. He found it relatively simple to get through all six statements. He had no trouble admitting that mom's decision was wrong, but he stalled for a few minutes on the thought of not defining Mom by her expectations. For years he had carried around the notion that Mom was an arrogant, self-centered individual who only cared about her agenda. Whenever he thought his way, he noticed that his heart hardened and his confidence dropped. He realized that this had a hold on him that he didn't want. He realized that she would have much less influence on him if he viewed her as an individual who needed God's grace just like he did. When he was able to see her as an imperfect human being rather than the powerful agenda setter of the family, she seemed to shrink right in front of his eyes.

4. Be patient and persistent. Forgiveness is more of a lifestyle than a one-time event. At any one sitting, it will probably be impossible to finish dealing with every situation that requires forgiveness. Therefore, forgiveness must be a process that you keep working on day after day. Deal with every situation you can handle today, but don't get frustrated because you can't dismiss every offense. Just deal with the ones you are ready for. Then give God ongoing permission to bring to your mind any situation needing forgiveness when he knows you are ready. Each time one of these situations comes to mind, walk it through the six statements to insure that the pain of harmful situations doesn't get a foothold in your heart.

Steven felt a lot better and more equipped to face the challenges of life after this commitment to forgive his mom, but he wasn't able to finish. He tried to apply the six statements to his mom's constant criticism, but he could tell he was only playing a game. Rather than go through the motions, he decided it was better to be honest and admit he was not ready. The criticism didn't seem quite as big as it used to with the other issues out of the way, but he just wasn't ready. He prayed and gave God permission to bring this to the surface when he was ready, but other than that he just put it out of mind and went on with his life.

About four months later, Steven was called into his supervisor's office just before work was done on Wednesday. She told him that she wanted to see him in her office first thing the next morning. She didn't say what it was about, but it was obvious she was intense about seeing him.

That night, Steven was miserable. An avalanche of thoughts descended upon his mind—and not one of them was positive. *She must be unhappy with my work. Am I going to get fired? Is the owner mad at me and ordering my supervisor to do his dirty work?* His inability to dismiss these negative thoughts created a sleepless, miserable night.

Exhausted, Steven went to the meeting with his supervisor expecting the worst. When his supervisor explained that the company was opening a new office and they wanted Steven to head up the project, he was relieved and angry all at once. He decided that day that Mom would no longer be a cloud hanging over his life. He had finally grown tired of her legacy of doom that was stealing the joy of anticipation from his heart. For the first time in his life he was able find the strength to forgive his mom and gain self-control over the influence from her that he wanted to keep and the influence that he wanted to dismiss.

5. Peel off the layers. You will find that bitterness gets put on in layers and comes off in layers. It is common for people to apply forgiveness to a situation and feel better for a short period of time, only to find they are upset again later. You may conclude when this happens that you have not actually forgiven. More likely you have just reached a new layer in the effects that the harmful event had on your life.

As Steven released himself from the negative influence Mom had over him, he began to notice other issues rising to the surface. In response to Mom's constant criticism, Steven had become a workaholic, spending long hours working to attempt to get Mom's approval.

This overcommitment to work was creating isolation in his relationship with his wife and family and was starting to affect his health. Steven realized he had to forgive his mom for developing this characteristic in him. Having done this, he realized he didn't trust any women who were the same age as his mom. He carried an emotional assumption that all women who were approximately thirty years older than he was would be critical and unyielding in their expectations. He began to realize that he was projecting a characteristic that was true about his mom on every woman in his life. As he worked through the process of forgiving his mom for creating this unrealistic assessment, he discovered that there were a lot of women who were genuinely interested in helping others and sincere in their love.

Having worked through the layers of bitterness with his mom, Steven discovered a surprising development in his heart. As his mom was cleared out of the way in his emotional life, Steven began to realize he had very little respect for his dad. Throughout the years, he had been building resentment over his dad's willingness to allow Mom to run him down and manipulate him. He had never faced this resentment because Mom was such an obvious issue in his life. He was never able to understand how a man could let a woman be so dominant and have such an unhealthy influence in the lives of his kids. Now that he was an adult, he was even more amazed that Dad was not willing to stand up for himself or anyone else in the house against Mom's barrages.

As he was willing to face this fact, he noticed a trend in his life. He had conveniently avoided developing any relationships with men his dad's age. He had unknowingly allowed his life to be shaped by a lack of trust in men who would be positive mentors in his life. There were significant deficiencies in his development as a result. He was able to function in business and carry on friendships, but he consistently fell short of reaching his goals and avoided opportunities that were challenging for him. He lacked the leadership confidence to reach his potential because he lacked a strong leadership example in his father and could not allow himself to replace his father with an adequate role model.

Steven thought he had grown up and was an independent individual. But as he seriously faced the issue of forgiveness he came to realize that he was timid about challenges, insecure about decision-making and cautious in vital relationships. He was never going to get out from under this influence accidentally. It would happen only by a deliberate decision on his part to adopt the positive qualities of his parents' lives and discard their negative influence.

Needless to say, he became less fearful of opening up to Sherry. He realized she did not give him the messages of inadequacy he had learned to expect. Sherry was not like Mom. The work Steven did in dealing with family patterns from his past paid off with new freedom, honesty and trust for Sherry and himself.

Focus on the Heart

Heavenly Father, please reveal to my mind any and all people who have hurt me and whom I have not forgiven. Give me the wisdom to see that nothing else will remove the pain from my heart—and the strength to truly forgive.

A Step Toward Love

Ask your spouse, "What is the easiest of the six statements of forgiveness for you to apply? What is the hardest?" Share your answers with your spouse, and then pray for each other a simple prayer such as "God, help my spouse master the process of forgiveness."

Six

Will You Forgive Me?

Once an individual has worked through the process of forgiveness and has reduced the bitterness of past hurts into motivation for further growth, the process of reconciliation and healthy interaction can begin for a couple. It is vitally important to make sure the pain of the past has been dealt with internally before this interaction happens. If the pain is still simmering like a dormant volcano, the conversations necessary to bring restoration will revive the pain and cause an eruption that will carve out a whole new path of destruction in your relationship.

Stephanie had put up with the disrespectful behavior of her husband for years, thinking she had somehow brought it upon herself. As she approached her fortieth birthday she decided she had had enough. She started attending a Bible study with a small group of women; it was focused on issues of personal growth. She learned the importance of self-respect and of setting boundaries that characterize relationships of respect. In the meantime, her husband, James, was beginning to do some soul-searching of his own. His kids from a previous marriage were making decisions that were troubling to him. That caused him to take a good look at his own decision-making and led him to commit to a Bible study with a small group of men. As a result, Stephanie had confidence that they could work things out if they could get some direction. She asked James to begin going to marriage counseling with her.

It didn't take long for a root problem to become clear: there was a lot of baggage from the past standing in the way of James and Stephanie's success in finding the kind of intimacy they wanted with each other. They attempted early in the process to talk through the abuses of the past. As they broached the subject, the wounds of the past broke open, and they began fighting once again. They were unable to rebuild any trust between them because they kept opening unhealed wounds.

She wanted to discuss his abusive language and the times he had thrown things at her. He wanted to leave it in the past and move on to other things. As a result, she felt he was living in denial, and he felt she just wanted to condemn him.

In retaliation, James brought up the fact that Stephanie had been sexually unresponsive throughout their marriage as a way of manipulating and punishing him. Stephanie saw the lack of sexually intimacy in their relationship as a result of their lack of caring communication. She didn't want to make a big deal out of it; she believed that sex would take care of itself if the rest of the relationship was working well. She felt condemned by James for not being able to dismiss this way of thinking. James felt that Stephanie did not really like him and no longer found him attractive.

What it came down to was this: James had never forgiven Stephanie, and Stephanie had never forgiven James. They had buried the issues, ignored the issues—but never *forgiven* each other for the issues. Now, when they then tried to discuss the issues, the thin film of denial peeled off and exposed a bleeding wound. In order to effectively discuss these issues, they would need to work through the process of forgiveness in their hearts. The pain of past hurts would have to be healed, and new convictions would have to be developed.

Preparing for the Conversation

To prepare for these tough conversations, you must first reach a place where you can talk in a secure way about what you want in your relationship. This definitely requires that the process of forgiveness be embraced. If the wound still has a scab on it, it can easily be ripped open. There may also need to be some sessions where anger is expressed, to see if the couple has the fortitude to withstand honest and courageous conversation. If one of the partners has been the victim in the situation, this is even more important. The wounded individual must have confidence that this will be a conversation of equals. For some couples this must be tested in honest, air-clearing interaction where the hurt individual feels permission to be honest.

In addition, each partner must have a clear idea of what kind of relationship they want. These convictions need to be embraced in a matter-of-fact way. You need to be able to discuss these desires in a way that is safe. If your convictions are embraced by your partner, it will bring joy to your heart. If your convictions are not embraced by your partner, it should not throw you into a tailspin. You will experience some disappointment, but you need to be secure enough in your boundaries that you will not be shaken by disagreement.

Make the Lists

To start the process of restoration, each spouse should make a list entitled "The Things for Which My Spouse Needs to Forgive Me." Include on this list the times you can think of where you have offended your spouse or done something that was wrong in regards to your relationship. Don't overanalyze your life and write down every little mistake you have ever made. That would put too much emphasis on you and make your spouse feel pity for you rather than love. You want to include the events that are strategic to the health of your relationship.

Then each of you should make a second list entitled "The Things for Which I Need to Forgive My Spouse." Include on this list the times when your spouse has offended you. Again, don't overanalyze your spouse, just be strategic. Don't rush either of these two lists. It would be good to start them and keep them active for a couple of weeks. That way you can add to them or modify them as you get used to the idea of rebuilding a relationship.

Check Your Heart

Once you get these two lists made, it is important to take time and ask yourself if you have forgiven each item on the list. For the first list, "The Things for Which My Spouse Needs to Forgive Me," ask yourself, "Have I asked God's forgiveness and then forgiven *myself* for each of these?" For the second list, "The Things for Which I Need to Forgive My Spouse," ask yourself, "Have I forgiven my spouse for each of these?"

Do not attempt to discuss the items on these lists with each other until you are confident that forgiveness has been found in your own heart! These lists are like explosives. They will either propel your relationship forward in a great step of growth or tear an even bigger hole in your heart. Make sure there is no gunpowder of bitterness below the surface, waiting to be ignited. Use the six statements of forgiveness in chapter five to test each of the concerns on your lists.

Read Between the Lines

Your lists of forgiveness contain clues to the expectations you have for your relationship. As you discuss these lists you are going to reveal to yourself, and hopefully to one another, these expectations. It is these expectations that form the basis for reorganizing your relationship so that both of you will be satisfied with the end result. Any work you can do ahead of time to discover and evaluate these expectations will expedite the process.

If your list has physical mistreatment on it, then it is obvious you expect physical safety and respect to be a part of your relationship. If your list includes the need to forgive your spouse for miscommunication and demanding his or her own agenda, you probably want a relationship where active and effective listening is a priority. If you think there has been a lack of understanding of your needs, you probably want to pursue honest conversation about the differences between men and women and how your needs get met as opposed to your spouse's. These expectations become the definition of the new relationship you hope to build together.

Consider the following example of Nathan and Kristie.

HUSBAND'S LIST 1: THE THINGS FOR WHICH MY SPOUSE NEEDS TO FORGIVE ME

1. I have been controlling with our finances.

IMPLICATION: I want a relationship of cooperation with money.

2. I allowed my anger to get out of control and hurt Kristie when I grabbed her arms.

IMPLICATION: I want a relationship where we are not angry with each other.

3. I missed our youngest daughter's dance recital because I wanted to play golf.

IMPLICATION: I want a relationship with a realistic schedule.

4. I had a one-night stand with a woman in another city on a business trip.

IMPLICATION: I want a mutually satisfying sexual relationship with my wife.

5. I have continually made Kristie feel guilty about the way she does things.

IMPLICATION: I want a relationship where we do not manipulate each other.

HUSBAND'S LIST 2: THE THINGS FOR WHICH I NEED TO FORGIVE MY SPOUSE

1. Kristie spends money without planning ahead—like the new bedroom furniture for the children.

IMPLICATION: I want a relationship of cooperation with money.

2. Kristie had a deep emotional relationship with a man at work that

almost became a sexual relationship.

IMPLICATION: I want a mutually satisfying sexual relationship with my wife.

3. Kristie uses anger to get her way—like the way she pushed for the vacation in Florida by angrily accusing me of not caring about the family.

IMPLICATION: I want a relationship where we do not manipulate each other.

4. Kristie refers to me with demeaning terms like "jerk," "lazy," "you're not a real man."

IMPLICATION: I want a relationship where we respect one another.

5. Kristie uses sex to manipulate me. If I do something for her, we have sex. If I refuse her anything, she refuses me sex.

IMPLICATION: I want a relationship where we do not manipulate each other.

IMPLICATION: I want a mutually satisfying sexual relationship with my wife.

WIFE'S LIST 1: THE THINGS FOR WHICH MY SPOUSE NEEDS TO FORGIVE ME

1. I got emotionally involved with Steve at work. I can't believe it almost became sexual.

IMPLICATION: I want a relationship where we are emotionally connected enough that I *want* to have sex with Nathan.

2. I spend money without thinking ahead because I am afraid that if I ask Nathan I will not get anything.

IMPLICATION: I want a relationship where we talk about money more often.

3. I sometimes find sex to be repulsive. When I don't feel totally loved by Nathan, I don't respond.

IMPLICATION: I want a relationship where we are emotionally connected enough that I *want* to have sex with him.

4. I have learned to be angry. I have said mean things about Nathan's manhood, and I have thrown a lot of tantrums.

IMPLICATION: I want a relationship where we respect each other.

5. I have been too focused on the kids' needs and have ignored Nathan's needs.

IMPLICATION: I want a relationship with a realistic schedule; I want a relationship where we sincerely care for each other.

WIFE'S LIST 2: THE THINGS FOR WHICH I NEED TO FORGIVE MY SPOUSE

1. Nathan has been too demanding. I don't seem to do anything right in his eyes. The house isn't clean enough. The kids aren't parented right. I don't take care of the car right and so on.

IMPLICATION: I want a relationship where we respect each other.

2. Nathan never communicates about money. I never know how much money we have or how much I can spend.

IMPLICATION: I want a relationship where we cooperate with money.

3. Nathan has been mad at me about Steve, but he had sex with another woman!

IMPLICATION: I want a relationship of deep trust where we can find sexual satisfaction with each other.

4. Nathan never communicates. When we try to talk he usually ends up angry—like the other night when we were talking about the kids' upcoming events and he blew up over all the demands on his time.

IMPLICATION: I want a relationship where we try to understand each other.

Share the First List

Check your attitude before this conversation and periodically throughout your interaction. Ask yourself, *Do I really want reconciliation? Am I willing to let my spouse back into my heart? Can I remember the good times of our relationship that I would like to recover? Am I willing to protect the investment I have made in our life together?* This process of sharing the shortcomings of life will give you power to hurt one another or access to healing. Which of these powerful positions you land in will be determined by your attitude.

Once both of you are confident that forgiveness is a reality in your heart, get together and each share your first list: "The Things for Which My Spouse Needs to Forgive Me." It is important to start with this list so you promote vulnerability. It is too easy to be accusatory with the second list. To promote healing, you must be willing to take responsibility for the mistakes you have made and give your spouse the opportunity to take responsibility for his or her mistakes. When you take responsibility for your shortcomings by apologizing and asking for forgiveness, you show your spouse you are interested in rebuilding the relationship rather than merely in justifying your actions. The process becomes a "visual aid" for your spouse. If you are vulnerable and humble, an environment of growth is encouraged. If you are self-protective, an environment of defensiveness is encouraged.

Ideally there will be no need to discuss your second lists. It is possible that everything on your second list is already on your spouse's first list, and dealing with the first lists first will have covered it. The first list requires a level of humility and self-disclosure that makes trust easier to build. The second list requires a great amount of tact as you bring up offenses that your spouse may not be willing to readily admit. The negotiation process requires a strong foundation of grace in order to succeed.

Be patient with the first list. Do not just read through it as if it were a shopping list that you are checking off as the items are purchased. Discuss one item at a time, and discuss it until you are confident that forgiveness has not only been offered but sincerely embraced in both of your hearts. Each of these items is an opportunity to develop intimacy in your relationship. If you rush through them you may leave the impression that you are trivializing the important issues of life.

Offer Grace

As your spouse shares the items on his or her first list, respond with encouragement and grace. Recognize that your partner is taking a courageous step of self-disclosure. This is probably going to be a vulnerable event—maybe the most difficult step your spouse will ever take in personal interaction with you.

In order to achieve healing, forgiveness needs to be shared back and forth. When your spouse asks, "Will you forgive me for . . . ?" respond with positive statements of encouragement. Your spouse is being vulnerable and needs to know that you are interested in a new relationship. Have patience with the process. This is just the first step of restoration. You are not justifying the harmful actions, and you are not settling for a future of mediocrity; you are simply forgiving. There is still repentance to be confirmed by action and a new track record of excellence to be established. Verbal forgiveness is just the first step that allows your spouse to get out of the dog house and back into the game.

Negotiate the Future

After offering forgiveness, the conversation should shift to a discussion of new expectations and boundaries for your relationship. As mentioned earlier, each of the areas needing forgiveness represents a desire in your hearts for change in your relationship. As you discover these desires you will start to draw a road map for renewal.

For repentance to be believable, there must be a growing track record of new behavior and a commitment to learning new life skills. The old patterns of interaction need to be worked on so that you do not wind up in the same place all over again. The purpose of reconciliation is to establish a new relationship, not give permission for the old relationship to continue. The two of you must learn to honestly and deliberately express your desires and negotiate new patterns for your relationship.

Start with activities that build credibility. Rebuilding trust in a relationship takes time and strategic thinking. The first activities of reconciliation are going to be stilted and overstated. The person who made the mistake or inflicted the pain will probably feel like too much is being expected, but it is a necessary first step. It does not mean that it will be like this for the rest of your life, but until credibility is reestablished, the relationship will need some extra help; don't worry if you feel awkward.

Defeat Unhealthy Habits

Your marriage may have been damaged by involvement in unhealthy habits such as pornography. John and Jeannie were excited when the promotion came through. John had been working hard at his career for ten years, and the opportunity to move into sales provided financial freedom for his family. At first the traveling was stimulating and encouraging. The new people he met and the sights he got to see around the country seemed to offset the time away from Jeannie and the kids. After a few months, however, the excitement wore off, and John became bored and lonely. He longed to have his family nearby but knew it was unrealistic. He wished for Jeannie to be there to talk to and share the experiences that had now become dull and uninteresting.

Out of boredom one night he bought an adult magazine—and found it to be stimulating. The thrill of life seemed to return as the magazine became his companion for the night. He justified his actions by telling himself, *It isn't hurting anybody. At least they are not real women— that would be worse. It only makes me want to be with Jeannie more.* These thoughts calmed his fears and guided him through the initial experience. When he left the hotel room he threw away the magazine. The sense of relief from knowing that Jeannie would never have to know made him all that much more interested in Jeannie. Although she was surprised by the heightened interest of her husband, she definitely was not disappointed that the love of her life found her exciting and desirable.

John told himself he would never do it again. But the next trip saw a repeat of the same performance. It seemed easier this time to buy the magazine because no harm had come out of the last experience. This time the justification progressed to include thoughts like, *It didn't cause any harm last time. In fact, Jeannie and I had one of the best times ever after my last trip. Maybe this is going to put a new spark in our relationship.* Once again John threw away the magazine before returning home, and Jeannie never knew why he was once again very amorous when he got home. At this point, John could see no harm in his new experience, and Jeannie was starting to think that absence really does make the heart grow fonder.

At that, the door was pushed wide open. John was fooled into thinking that pornography was actually helping his marriage. Jeannie had her senses turned off because she enjoyed the attention she was getting from her rejuvenated husband. It didn't take long before John started watching adult movies in his hotel room and purchasing more graphic material.

As the intensity of the pornography increased, John became painfully aware that Jeannie would never be interested in the acts he was now viewing on a regular basis. Although he found them stimulating, he knew she would find them revolting and degrading. Rather than coming home from trips rejuvenated and eager to make love with Jeannie, he was now angry—and disappointed in his wife. When Jeannie would ask why he was coming home anxious and angry rather than energetic like before, he would just say that things were stressful and demanding.

He knew in his heart that he was keeping a destructive secret from Jeannie, but he was afraid to come clean. If he confessed the pornography he would have to give it up, and it seemed like his only release from the constant demands. But if he didn't confess his new habit, he would continue to interrupt his love life with a wife who had been very good to him. He was even nagged by the realization that he had thought Jeannie was a good lover before he got involved with pornography. Now that he compared her to the rehearsed acts of passion he was watching on videos, he viewed her with a disappointment that she didn't deserve.

John was jolted back into reality one Friday when one of his Monday business trips was transferred to another salesman. John's boss approached him and said, "John, you have been doing extremely well, and we would like to promote you to sales manager. As a result, some of your customers will be transferred to others so you can move into a position of management."

John exploded with anger, "You can't do that. That is my account.

Those are my people. You can't just turn them over to someone else. Why didn't you talk to me sooner about this?"

John's boss didn't understand why John had reacted so violently. John was having a great amount of success, and the boss assumed he would be flattered by the promotion. He assumed John must be under a lot of pressure, so he said to him, "Why don't you go home early today and take the weekend to cool off. We'll talk about this Monday. You seem to be under a lot of pressure—maybe you just need some rest."

John packed his things and drove home. At first he was seething over the decision his boss had made without his permission. But as he got closer to home, the real source of his anger set in. He was mad because he would have to stay home next week. He had planned on being gone and had already planned his rendezvous with his imaginary lovers. Now his plans had been interrupted.

The realization hit him like a load of bricks. He instantly knew he needed to take drastic actions. He could no longer live his life silently chasing relationships that didn't exist. When he arrived home he was quiet and introspective. When he asked Jeannie for time on Saturday night to talk, she was intrigued. They went out to dinner.

John started the conversation awkwardly. "Jeannie, there's something I need to talk with you about. It is very hard to get started because I know you are going to be hurt and disappointed."

"What is it, John? You haven't had an affair, have you?" Jeannie said it lightly. But when John didn't laugh and looked down at the table, she felt a chill run through her.

"No, I haven't had an affair. Not really," John said quietly, with embarrassment in his voice.

"What do you mean, not really?" Jeannie asked nervously.

"You remember when I got the promotion to being a salesman and we were all excited. Well, it was the best move to date in my career, but it was probably the worst move in my personal life. You probably won't be able to forgive me, but here goes anyway. I have been getting increasingly involved in pornography since about four months after I started traveling. It started innocently enough, but it has become a big enough problem that I was angry when my trip for next week was canceled. I never meant to hurt you. I love you more than anyone else on earth. I hope you can forgive me and together we can work on this, but I wouldn't blame you if you stayed angry at me for a long time. I only know I can't live with this secret any longer."

Jeannie sat at the table in stunned silence. She looked down at her plate, then up at John, then at the wall, then at John and then back at her plate again.

"Aren't you going to say anything?" John asked.

"I don't know what to say," Jeannie offered quietly. "I feel astonished; I feel violated. And yet I'm glad you told me. No, I wish you had never told me! Oh, I don't know what I wish. I just wish this had never happened."

For the rest of the evening Jeannie sat silently seething over what she considered to be a lack of self-control on John's part. John sat silently in ashamed resignation. It took months for Jeannie to work though her own hurt with the help of a supportive group of women and some counseling with an insightful Christian professional. During that time John started meeting with a supportive group of men for Bible study and prayer and went through his own counseling process. Jeannie decided she would forgive John, but she also recognized that things would have to change if she was going to have confidence in John again.

They mutually agreed on some activities that would help rebuild John's credibility in her eyes. He began attending a group for men focused on the issues of sexual addiction. He approached his boss and accepted the promotion to sales manager, which required only minimal trips and no traveling alone. In addition, John agreed, for a six-month period, to call when he left work so Jeannie would know he was not getting distracted by any temptations on the way home. John also asked his Bible study group to ask him weekly how his struggle with pornography was going so that he had some extra accountability. These would not become permanent aspects of their relationship, but they did help instill a sense of renewal and showed Jeannie that John was serious about changing and defeating this habit in his life.

Focus on the Heart
Lord of the heart, please give my spouse the grace to forgive me for the things I have done to interrupt our relationship. I know I cannot erase the past, and I don't want to inflict any more hurt. Please neutralize the foolishness of my past by giving my spouse a forgiving heart.

A Step Toward Love
Use the forgiveness lists from this chapter to determine the positive convictions you have about how a married couple can be healthy. Then use these convictions to write a positive description of the kind of relationship you would like to have with your spouse.

After you have written it, have a couple of friends read it to make sure you are not just dumping a lot of unrealistic expectations on your spouse and sabotaging your success. If your friends give you the green light, give it to your spouse with a prayer that it will open up a new level of communication.

For example, you may be irritated that your wife spends money without discussing it first, she unloads her emotional stress on you in verbal outbursts, and she refuses to allow your children to be out of her sight long enough for the two of you to get away alone. The positive convictions you hold are that married couples should coordinate their financial decisions, they should protect one another emotionally and they should continue building their life of intimacy after they have children. Your letter could be something like this:

Dear _____,

I am glad to be married to you. And I am committing myself today to build a relationship with you where we cooperate financially, emotionally and sexually.

I will consult you on any significant use of our money. I will protect your heart from the struggles of life as often as I can. I will seek for time to spend with just you so we can fall in love over and over again.

Please join me on this journey. I love you, and I look forward to the rest of our life together.

Seven

Reconciling
Our Differences

Between them they have had eight marriages, but now they run a marriage-repair ministry called Reconciling God's Way. How can a couple with such a bad track record learn to forgive, to trust and to love again?

About one and a half years into Joe and Michelle Williams's marriage, Michelle felt like her love for Joe had died. A few years later they separated. During this lonely period, they each made a commitment to Jesus and thought they'd found a quick fix to their marriage problems. Eight months of separation ended with a renewal ceremony in front of their new church. They thought things were looking up. However, just a few months later, Joe and Michelle were again separated.

Frustrated, Joe marched into his pastor's office pounding his fist on the desk. "I know we embarrassed you. I know we've embarrassed ourselves. I know divorce isn't an option. What are you going to do with us? God has to have an answer, right?"

They found themselves taking turns wanting reconciliation. Through the counsel of their church, they each chose to meet with older believers. Joe met with a small group of men while Michelle chose to be discipled by two older women, one of whom she walked with each day. They both decided to steer clear of singles groups because they were living in a nomad's land somewhere between marriage and singleness.

"Our focus had been too much on one another," remembers Joe. "I was Michelle's god and she mine. We kept trying to appease one another—and it wasn't working."

Michelle was looking for a biblical way out. One day a friend mentioned that she thought Joe flirted. Michelle thought she had found her way out; she filed for divorce. On a morning walk with the woman who was discipling her, Michelle shared her decision to divorce. Her friend stopped in her tracks. "That isn't a good enough reason, Michelle. That is in clear violation of the Bible." Michelle was devastated.

"I stopped in the middle of the road and burst into tears," Michelle said. "My friend wrapped her arms around me. Even though it hurt and I didn't feel like it, I decided to obey God and not divorce Joe."

Michelle found herself ambivalent toward Joe. Some days were filled with anger and frustration. Other days ushered in a flood of loneliness and longing for him. On one of those days of loneliness, Michelle showed up on the steps of Joe's apartment wanting to be held.

Joe said, "Michelle, I can't take this anymore. You keep sweeping in and out of my life. I'm sorry, but you can't come in." With that Joe calmly shut the door.

Michelle was hurt and angry. Driving home she was thinking how cold and uncaring Joe had been. All she wanted was his friendship. She longed to be held. Suddenly, Michelle sensed a strong presence of God and felt that God was saying to her, "Michelle, you keep running to the arms of men. I want to comfort you. I have been holding my arms out to you. Come to me." That night Michelle spent much time in prayer and Bible study and felt a sure peace. She continued that pattern of spending large amounts of time daily asking God to meet her.

In the midst of Michelle's personal revival, God was also working on Joe's heart. All his efforts to make the relationship work had gone bankrupt. In desperation Joe prayed, "God, my life is yours. I'll do it your way. I'll trust you with this relationship."

A short time later Michelle had to travel out of town, and Joe borrowed her car because his was in the shop. When Joe picked Michelle up at the airport, she noticed that something had changed.

"He seemed different, but I couldn't tell you why. He asked how I was doing, and then he invited me to go to lunch on Sunday. In my surprise I said yes. We spent all day Sunday together. I went from having no feelings toward Joe to feeling madly in love—in one day!

"Months before, in a quiet time with God, I had made a list of six things that would convince me Joe had changed. I had decided that I would go back to him if I saw those things in his life. They were things such as asking about the kids, wondering how I was doing financially, telling me I could continue to grow as a person—things like that. On that Sunday we were together, he did all six things on the list!"[1]

Build Healthy Habits

For the couple who wants to hold their relationship together after it has been violated, reconciliation is a courageous and scary process. Obstacles stand in the way of even the most willing couple. In order to navigate the treacherous seas of reconciliation, each couple must develop a game plan that protects them from further damage while they wrestle with the issue of reuniting.

Many couples develop problems in their relationship because they do not establish and maintain healthy behaviors in their personal lives. Joe and Michelle were one of these couples. Joe was angry with Michelle because she failed to meet his unrealistic expectations. He admits, "I thought that her desire to meet all my needs meant that she loved me. I had unrealistic expectations of her, and when she let me down I felt unloved and rejected by her."[2]

Schedule Time Together

Couples allow the demands of their life to dictate their schedules to the point that couple time gets eliminated. We are all busy. The kids are screaming in our ears to meet their needs. Our jobs demand that we give long hours for short pay. Our churches need us to volunteer our time and talents. Our own needs are silently yearning to be noticed. Whatever captures our time will own our hearts. Joe and Michelle needed a plan that would deliberately put them in situations that fostered intimacy and promoted communication.

Most couples think that communication will happen spontaneously and that the time for talking will be obvious. But life's demands will quickly squeeze out the time you have as a couple to get to know one another and coordinate your life. If you allow communication to develop accidentally you will most likely have a relationship filled with accidents. Instead, develop a deliberate method for staying in touch.

Plan regular meetings with one another where you discuss the issues of life. At this meeting, talk about money concerns, schedule demands, the needs of the kids and your own personal well-being. Ask questions such as "How are you doing with the demands of our life?" "Are you becoming vulnerable to any specific temptations?" "Are you feeling weak in any areas of life?" "What are some specific things I can pray about for you?" The purpose of this meeting is to sort out the decisions of your life and maintain the proper amount of accountability with one another so your life runs as stress-free as possible. If you can stay on top of the responsible side of life in a disciplined way, you are much more likely to enjoy your couple time together.

Foster Intimate Communication

Pragmatic conversations about the necessities of life keep things operating, but they do little to foster intimacy. In addition to deliberate business meetings, a wise couple will schedule regular dates to focus on themselves as a couple. This should be time away from the interruptions of kids and life's demands. It can be hard to find this time, but it is a lot easier than hearing one day that another person is vying for your spouse's love.

The secret to intimate conversation is to ask personal questions and listen to the responses. We are prone to jumping into our spouse's answers with our own brilliant analysis, which severs the ability to truly look into the heart of the one we love. When you resist the temptation to change one another and commit instead to the ongoing discovery of each other, the payoff is remarkable. Emotionally, your hearts beat together. Intellectually, you admire the contribution your differences bring to your family life. Socially, you are proud to be seen in public together. Physically, you enjoy an active and satisfying sexual life together.

The only way to develop this kind of connection is to communicate. You need to take turns listening to one another, patiently exploring your perspective on the questions of life. For help in finding questions to discuss, see *The Question Book* by Dennis and Barbara Rainey or our books *Love to Love You, Let Her Know You Love Her* or *Love to Love You Love Talk Box.*

Michelle remembers, "I didn't know how to discuss my fears and feelings with him, so I would withdraw or lash out in anger at the least little things. The funny thing is that the whole six weeks that we sat in that pastor's office arguing, God was using the process to allow me to bring my fears and issues out in the open, which ultimately saved our marriage! Sometimes the pastor left us alone to argue while he waited out in the hall, so it wasn't necessarily that I felt safer with a third party present. It was that I finally took the risk to get everything out in the open."[3]

Safeguard Meetings with Individuals of the Opposite Sex

Married people often get careless and think another person could never get a foothold in their hearts. As a result they get lazy about safeguarding time spent with someone of the opposite sex. Meetings between men and women are necessary and desirable in the flow of our lives. Business meetings are more stimulating when the perspective of both sexes is included. Churches are more relevant to the whole community when male and female input is integrated into the planning. Family life is richer when your family can get together with other families and have healthy interaction. Your perspective into your spouse's needs can be enhanced by input from someone of the opposite sex who is safe. But to keep these relationships healthy you must set boundaries, emanating out of your reservoir of self-respect.

Our suggestion is that you do not spend time alone with members of the opposite sex—have someone else present who is relevant to the conversation. Do not bring someone else in awkwardly by saying, "I can't be alone with you; there needs to be someone else here." This makes you look paranoid and unable to handle life on your own. Say, "I think we should have John join us because this affects him too." If the other person is unwilling to have another person present, politely respond, "I'm not really comfortable with that; are there any other options?" If the person demands that you spend time alone together, watch out. Affairs often begin as innocent meetings about simple issues related to work or mutual friends and then escalate to the point where hearts are knitted together.

At those times when it is impossible or impractical to have another person present, make sure someone else knows you are meeting. For instance, if a woman drops by my office unexpectedly, I will call Pam and say, "Janet just dropped by the office. I will be talking with her for about fifteen minutes, and then I'll be home." I make sure Janet hears me say this and is politely put on alert that my relationship with Pam is more important than anything she might need to talk about. (I also make sure to leave the office door open.) This can seem like a needless hassle and may usually be unnecessary, but the security it provides for your heart and your spouse is well worth the investment.

Pursue Individual Growth

Too often, couples put off personal growth while they are working toward progress in their marital relationship. But conflict exists in the marriage precisely because you and your spouse are missing certain skills or character traits that would make your relationship successful. If you do not mature, you will be powerless to bring anything new into your interaction. Personal growth is a lifelong pursuit. Most local churches offer Sunday-school classes or small group Bible studies that foster individual growth. Any Christian bookstore will contain numerous books that address the issues of personal growth. Your local Christian radio station airs quality programming that recommends resources on a regular basis. Take some time to listen. When you connect with a certain program, order the resources they are offering and begin feeding your mind with new information.

Joe and Michelle came to grips with this vital step to reconciliation while they were separated. "Before our separation," Michelle states confidently, "anytime one of us wanted to participate in an activity that didn't include the other, it was seen as a threat. When we reconciled, we both realized that all the little interests we had added in our lives made us more fulfilled individuals—and actually made us more attractive to the other."

Joe adds, "I realize now that all those times that Michelle wanted time alone to think, write, read, or go off somewhere to 'spend some time with God,' it wasn't because she didn't enjoy my company. . . . I see now how important it is for us to be individuals."[4]

If you are struggling in your relationship, it is likely there are some characteristics present in you that are damaging to your spouse, your personal well-being and the health of your marriage. If you do not address these traits with aggressive personal growth, they will continue to eat away at your relationship. Joe and Michelle discovered in their growth process that anger was a weapon they used against each other.

Joe candidly admits, "Each time we argued, I became so frustrated that I actually ended up saying and doing the exact opposite of what I knew I should. I'd say something that triggered some feeling or thought in Michelle, and she'd explode. When she would get angry with me I'd never know what to expect. Sometimes she'd break something, other times she'd say things that I couldn't believe could come out of her mouth."

Michelle agrees, "When I would tell Joe something I disagreed with him about, he'd get so irritated with me that I just got in to the habit of not saying anything . . . so in my desire to keep peace and have things run smoothly at home I just stuffed my feelings. Then, as Joe explained, when he least expected it, over some trivial matter, I'd blow."[5]

Many couples will identify with Joe and Michelle because anger is such a common characteristic of couples in conflict. Anger is like a spotlight that clearly illuminates areas of life that need to be changed. Michelle's grasp of this truth set the race for freedom off to a running start. "I read everything I could get my hands on concerning anger . . . putting much of the information I'd learned into practice, I felt a real sense of freedom. I no longer was afraid of anger—and it wasn't a lurking monster waiting to devour me anymore. Anger really was my friend. I knew that God had given me the emotion of anger to help me identify things I needed to change in my life."[6]

Promote Personalities

Other couples live with an undercurrent of irritation in their relationship because of a lack of understanding of the differences in personalities. There are many books worth studying on the differences among basic personalities.[7]

Most people marry a person who has a different personality from theirs. This makes for good variety. But it also makes for guaranteed conflict, because the two of you will want to do things differently! The success with which you manage your personality differences will determine how harmoniously your relationship works. Some people actually manage to marry someone like themselves and find a very high level of mutual understanding. They also discover they are no better at dealing with the nuances of life as married people than they were as singles, because the gaps that existed in their individual lives now exist in their marriage relationship. These couples need to work hard at learning creative ways to fill the gaps that are not covered by either personality.

In order to take advantage of differences in personality, you must first *accept one another's unique personality mix.* Michelle says that coming to this realization was one of the things that made their reconciliation possible.

> Joe was determined to put fun into our marriage, and I was goal-driven and wanted us to accomplish things. Then one Sunday we happened to see some tapes on the different temperament styles, and it changed our marriage and home life forever. . . . I realized Joe's unique difference from me was the way God had designed him and that it was OK for him to not be so goal-oriented.

Joe adds,

> Before I learned about the temperaments . . . I couldn't understand why she was always so driven to get things accomplished. . . . Now I don't get irritated with her when she's setting goals and serving in leadership positions—I see it as a strength and not as a threat.[8]

Your spouse cannot change the basic personality that came with birth. Growth and maturity can fill some of the gaps, but the basic personality cannot be picked out any more than height or eye color can be chosen. As you begin to see the benefits of your spouse's personality rather than focus on the irritations of living with someone different from you, you will notice traits and actions that your spouse brings to the marriage that you could never accomplish on your own.

The second step is to *divide responsibilities based on personality.* Any family's lifestyle has many facets. There are decision-making and goal-setting activities. There are daily responsibilities and long-range plans. There are social engagements and work requirements. There are housekeeping tasks and child-rearing imperatives. A wise couple takes the time to decide who should lead in each of these responsibilities based on natural abilities. Dividing the tasks of life in a way that doesn't match personalities guarantees that everyone in the family will be consistently under stress. Life in the home will be more strenuous. Each individual will lack confidence. All family members will experience constant fatigue. As a result, your relationship will be strained, and intimacy will be elusive.

For the gaps in your specific personality mix, hard work will have to substitute for the natural ability of the personalities. In this case, pray for strength and wisdom as you tackle the challenges. But as much as possible, divide the responsibilities of your life according to the natural abilities and personalities God has given you.

Third, *become a student of your spouse's sources of motivation.* Your unique mixture of personality traits results in natural motivation in some arenas of life and lack of motivation in others. Your spouse, likewise, finds some areas of life easily motivating while other areas are frustrating. The more time you spend in the areas of your natural motivation, the more effective life will be. If your spouse also spends most of the time in his or her areas of natural motivation, stress in your relationship will be reduced and your energy level as a couple will be increased.

Areas of motivation can be organized into the four categories described below. Practice each of the motivation techniques and take notice of which brings the best response from your spouse.

1. Your spouse is probably motivated by *control of decisions that affect his or her life* if he or she responds positively to

☐ leadership in decision-making

☐ freedom to give an opinion

☐ options to choose from

☐ direct statements like "I want to go out Friday to our favorite restaurant," "I want to meet with you on Wednesday to discuss our next vacation," "I'm upset with you and I need to talk with you."

2. Your spouse is probably motivated by *new relationships and new experiences* if he or she responds positively to

☐ spontaneous plans

☐ praise from you in the presence of other people

☐ meeting new people

☐ enthusiastic compliments like "You are so fun to be with!" "I love your new ideas." "My life would be boring without you."

3. Your spouse is probably motivated by *predictability and structure* if

he or she responds positively to

☐ traditions in your family

☐ an easy enough schedule to complete all tasks that are started

☐ predictable schedule and routine dates

☐ promises that are kept precisely as stated

4. Your spouse is probably motivated by *respect for who he or she is,* apart from tasks, if he or she responds positively to

☐ low expectations

☐ slow conversations

☐ statements of acceptance like "I'm glad you are in my life," "Our relationship works well because of your easy-going nature," "I like just being with you."

Once you have determined the responses that best motivate, practice encouraging your spouse strategically. Deliberately try using words and actions that you think will motivate your spouse to enjoy life with you. Keep practicing until it becomes second nature to you. While you are seeking to motivate your spouse, work on keeping yourself motivated as well. Review the decisions you have made in your life and ask yourself, *Do these decisions motivate or demotivate me?* Decide that your future decisions will be aimed at making your life easier to keep up with by lining up your life as much as possible with the natural abilities of your personality. Finally, every day for a month, thank God that your spouse has strengths that you do not have. Ask God to use these strengths to effectively fill the gaps in your life and to free you up to use your best traits to help make your family work.

Do Not Be Naive

You cannot bring health to your relationship by naively neglecting the areas that need change. You cannot ignore the issues and hope they will not affect your life. The pain you feel each time you are criticized cannot be buried. The sources of conflict in your marriage must be quieted with good communication skills. The hope that they will automatically be healed by the passing of time is seldom realized. What happens is that bad habits give rise to more bad habits that eventually make your relationship deteriorate into something neither of you ever signed up for.

The book of Genesis tells the history of Abram (later named Abraham) and Sarai (later named Sarah). Abraham was a man who moved often, sometimes in response to God's leading in his life and sometimes in response to life's circumstances. Sarah faithfully followed his lead and cooperated with his plans. One of these moves was brought about by a very natural fear.

> There was a famine in the land, and Abram went down to Egypt to live there for a while because the famine was severe. (Gen 12:10)

As Abram considered the move and the obstacles involved, he let fear get the best of him. Sarai's beauty mixed with the ruthlessness of the Egyptians replaced Abram's usual wisdom with ridiculous speculation about the future. He said to Sarai,

> I know what a beautiful woman you are. When the Egyptians see you, they will say, "This is his wife." Then they will kill me but will let you live. Say you are my sister, so that I will be treated well for your sake and my life will be spared because of you. (vv. 11-13)

Abram ignored the obvious turmoil that would inundate their lives if they played this scenario out.

> When Abram came to Egypt, the Egyptians saw that she was a very beautiful woman. And when Pharaoh's officials saw her, they praised her to Pharaoh, and she was taken into his palace. He treated Abram well for her sake, and Abram acquired sheep and cattle, male and female donkeys, menservants and maidservants, and camels. (vv. 14-16)

Abram allowed his wife to be taken into a harem by another man! Did he believe that physical safety would erase the emotional trauma Sarai was sure to experience? Did he expect Sarai to accept her role as a pawn for bargaining without being deeply hurt? Apparently, Abram naively thought this plan would work. In his grace, God intervened and brought about Sarai's release.

> But the LORD inflicted serious diseases on Pharaoh and his household

because of Abram's wife Sarai. So Pharaoh summoned Abram. "What have you done to me?" he said. "Why didn't you tell me she was your wife? Why did you say, 'She is my sister,' so that I took her to be my wife? Now then, here is your wife. Take her and go!" Then Pharaoh gave orders about Abram to his men, and they sent him on his way, with his wife and everything he had. (Gen 12:17-20)

You would think that such a close call would have brought Abram to attention. The near disaster should have awakened his senses and created an intense motivation to prohibit any repeat performances. But apparently he thought that time would just erase the flaw, or maybe he thought the same circumstances would never again present themselves, so there was no reason to give this inconsistency focused attention. Instead, the neglect incubated the desire to rely on such thinking again.

For a while [Abraham] stayed in Gerar, and there Abraham said of his wife Sarah, "She is my sister." Then Abimelech king of Gerar sent for Sarah and took her. (Gen 20:1-2)

Here he is doing it again! Sarah is once again put in harm's way so that Abraham will be safe. The first time can almost be recorded as inexperience, but the second time constitutes a true flaw in character. When Abimelech directly asks Abraham, "What was your reason for doing this?" (20:10), Abraham's response shows how he placed his well-being over Sarah's.

I said to myself, "There is surely no fear of God in this place, and they will kill me because of my wife." Besides, she really is my sister, the daughter of my father though not of my mother; and she became my wife. And when God had me wander from my father's household, I said to her, "This is how you can show your love to me: Everywhere we go, say of me, 'He is my brother.'" (Gen 20:11-13)

If Abraham and Sarah are to experience growth in their relationship, she is going to have to forgive abundantly and he is going to have to commit to treating her with honesty and respect. It is obvious as you read the Bible account that Abraham and Sarah navigated these stormy waters to develop a productive and encouraging marriage.

From Generation to Generation

But it is also obvious that Abraham never completely eliminated this
naiveté from his thinking. The amazing result is that the inconsistency
in the life of Abraham surfaces years later in the thinking of his son
Isaac.

> Now there was a famine in the land—besides the earlier famine of
> Abraham's time—and Isaac went to Abimelech king of the Philistines
> in Gerar.
>
> When the men of that place asked him about his wife, he said, "She is
> my sister," because he was afraid to say, "She is my wife." He thought,
> "The men of this place might kill me on account of Rebekah, because she
> is beautiful."
>
> When Isaac had been there a long time, Abimelech king of the Phi-
> listines looked down from a window and saw Isaac caressing his wife
> Rebekah. So Abimelech summoned Isaac and said, "She is really your
> wife! Why did you say, 'She is my sister'?"
>
> Isaac answered him, "Because I thought I might lose my life on
> account of her."
>
> Then Abimelech said, "What is this you have done to us? One of the
> men might well have slept with your wife, and you would have brought
> guilt upon us."
>
> So Abimelech gave orders to all the people: "Anyone who molests
> this man or his wife shall surely be put to death." (Gen 26:1, 7-11)

Now we see Rebekah in the same dilemma as Sarah. Her husband
is willing to put her in a treacherous situation so that he will remain
safe. Like father, like son! The love of Rebekah and Isaac for one
another is unmistakable, but it can only be kept alive by Rebekah's
willingness to forgive Isaac under very difficult circumstances.

Abraham and Isaac are two heroes of the Old Testament, but both
set themselves up for disaster. Only by God's direct and gracious intervention was each of them (and his wife) rescued. Even the best people
are capable of dark decisions, so we must all be alert. Forgiveness and

growth are indispensable ingredients to a healthy marriage. Naive neglect on our part will not only affect our own lives but also reproduce itself in subsequent generations.

As Joe and Michelle walked through the struggle of building a marriage of joy and support, Joe embraced this insight: "One time I heard someone say, 'You choose to do what you choose to do,' and I guess I finally came to an understanding that if I were ever going to be the man God had intended for me to be, it had to start with my making the right choices."[9]

Michelle said humility was the biggest change she saw in both of their lives. "We needed a new focus. At one point I went to Joe and asked him to forgive me for not being the wife he needed. It seemed to diffuse Joe. He expressed it best when he brought us each home an extra wedding band."

"This is to remind us that God is first in each of our lives," Joe added, "then comes each other."[10]

By making God his first priority, Joe discovered the ability to encourage Michelle in her personal growth. He actively cheered her on to develop her talents apart from him. As a result Michelle is no longer feeling smothered or trapped and is finding it possible to love her husband freely once again.

Focus on the Heart

Oh God my Maker, thank you for making my spouse so different from me. At times I wish we were more alike, but then I realize I don't need another me in my life. Help us both to be our best. Rescue us from the thought that we can attain excellence in our relationship through mediocre means.

A Step Toward Love

Make a list of all the ways you can think of in which your spouse is different from you. After each characteristic write a couple of advantages this difference brings to your family. Choose two or three of these characteristics to mention to your spouse in a note thanking him or her for being a gift from God to you.

Eight

Rebuilding Trust

S*even years of living hell,"* Ginny *said, "to get a marriage remade by* heaven. When there is that kind of hurt, it takes time for God to rebuild a relationship. Most people quit and give up too soon. People want instant fixes, but hearts aren't repaired that way. It takes years of daily hurt to tear a marriage apart, and it takes years of daily love to rebuild the trust. But it is possible—look at us!"

"Ginny and I had both been married before," added Carl. "We had bad habits going into the marriage. But I thought I was on top of the world, that I could handle anything: our relationship, our home. At work I was climbing the corporate ladder at a rapid-fire pace, so I thought I was invincible—but I wasn't. I found myself in an affair with a woman at work, and I was so full of myself that I thought I was entitled to it!"

Trust is the vital link between two people that allows intimacy to grow. Without trust, a man will never allow himself to move into the areas of emotional insight that draw his wife to him. Without trust a

woman will place demands on her husband to be faithful and responsible rather than sharing her heart in an appealing way. These become
especially treacherous slopes to climb if there is a past record of hurt or
disappointment. And the path of trust can be especially slippery if the
man and woman are not vulnerable people as individuals. In a
dynamic, growing relationship with Christ there is the strength to
become a secure, transparent person.

Trusting God First

For me (Bill), the willingness to risk honest disclosure was primarily
developed in a growing relationship with Jesus Christ. At sixteen
years old I recognized that I needed help in my life that was bigger
than me. I had seen the movie *The Exorcist,* and my eyes opened to the
reality of the spiritual world that is operating around us. I realized for
the first time that life is an interactive experience between the world
we can see and the world we cannot see.

I began reading the Bible to find answers and strength, and after
about a month I came across these words: "You, dear children, are
from God and have overcome them, because the one who is in you is
greater than the one who is in the world" (1 Jn 4:4). For some reason,
the light went on for me. I realized that night that I needed Jesus *inside*
my life. I needed him to dwell in me just as my soul does. I don't understand how my soul resides in my body, but I am fully aware of its presence through my personality and emotional reactions to life. In the
same way, I needed Jesus to be in me.

As time has passed, I have come to realize that Jesus can address
every need in my life because he lives inside me. I love Pam, but she
doesn't live inside me. I have some great friends, but they do not live
inside. Only Jesus can meet the needs that start inside me. I have discovered that he is the only one who can bring times of honest security.
He has adopted me into his family and made me an heir of his inheritance. He has said, "Never will I leave you; never will I forsake you"
(Heb 13:5). He has promised to give me a life that is abundant.

And I have discovered this: "If God is for us, who can be against

us? He who did not spare his own Son, but gave him up for us all—
how will he not also, along with him, graciously give us all things?"
(Rom 8:31-32). During those times when I can grasp the stability of a
growing relationship with Christ, I gain the ability to be a truly vulnerable individual who is not dependent on the acceptance of others to be
secure.

Instead of learning to trust God, we often load up our spouses with
unrealistic expectations. Many husbands think their wives can please
them in all things. We want them to always look good, always be sensitive and reasonable and always be responsive to our advances. Many
wives think their husbands should be strong leaders who always provide patient direction, financial security and emotional support. We
assign to our spouses needs that only God can meet. When a couple
turns this formula around and trusts God first, the pressure on the
marriage is eased and the chances for success are higher.

Carl and Ginny had fallen into this trap and finally realized they
could make things right only with God's help. Ginny reminisces,

> We married in 1978, but by 1982 I knew our marriage was in deep
> trouble. I remember praying, *God, do whatever you want to straighten me
> out. I give my marriage and myself to you.* Things with Carl got worse. The
> affair was exposed, and he moved out on Christmas Day! He moved
> home again for a short while, then moved out again on Valentine's Day!
> The first day Carl moved out (while I was at work), my sister came to
> tell me. I went to my desk, opened my Bible and read, "God is our ref-
> uge and strength, an ever-present help in trouble" (Ps 46:1), "Be still,
> and know that I am God" (Ps 46:10) and "'Because he loves me,' says
> the LORD, 'I will rescue him'" (Ps 91:14).
>
> I didn't know what that rescue would look like, but I knew I needed
> God to do it. I read that God wanted to be my counselor, so I vowed
> then and there to stay connected to God and do exactly what he asked
> me to do, when he asked me to do it. Over the next few months I read
> the whole Bible. When I read about the people in the Old Testament, I
> prayed *God, give me faith like that.* Somehow I knew that I needed God to
> change me. I couldn't do a thing about Carl, so I placed him in God's

hands. I concentrated on trusting God's timing with Carl and letting God change me.

Carl moved in and out three times. Ginny continued to read the Bible regularly and tried to apply what she was reading to her everyday life. Her personal confidence and sense of security were gradually growing. Finally she took a big step.

> I became convinced that Carl needed me to say, "You may not come home until you give her up." After I said it, he packed his bags and left. When he was gone, I noticed that he had taken the Bible I had given him. Carl hadn't believed in God up until that time. In fact, at times he mocked me for my beliefs.
>
> I knew God had asked me to give him time with Carl. And Carl had asked me to 'give him some space.' I knew what God wanted me to do—surrender. I prayed, *OK Lord, I am willing to be alone. I am willing to love tough. I am willing to do whatever you ask. Block me from saying what doesn't need said. Help me to say what does need said. Whatever you want Lord, I trust you, I trust your love, I trust your time.*

Learning to Trust Yourself

The next obstacle to the reconciliation of a relationship is a lack of confidence in the skills of your own life. Carl had a terrible time getting back together with Ginny and staying with her because he lacked the skills to make it work. There was too much pressure in the relationship. Ginny's needs would surface, and Carl would immediately be overwhelmed by them. He didn't know how to encourage her, so he responded awkwardly or ran away. Here are six skills that are vital to the success of any growing marriage. With practice, you can learn to do them!

1. Focus on changing yourself. Probably the most important skill for the success of relationships is the ability to look humbly at life. It is always easier to see other people's faults than our own. We seem to have emotional microscopes to use in evaluating the deficiencies of our spouses and telescopes to evaluate our own. We are reluctant to make changes in our own lives—but anxious for changes to take place in our spouses! The ability to focus on the need for change in *me* sets up the whole relationship for change.

Telling someone to change is unlikely to have any effect. Changing in the presence of your spouse and putting your example on display may be a key factor in your spouse's beginning to change as well.

2. Process the past. The events of your past form the story of your life. But it is more like a novel than a news report. You have added your interpretation, your emotional reactions and your commentary. As a result, the story you carry about your life deeply affects your functioning in life. It sets the emotional climate, just as a thermostat determines the temperature in your house.

The key is that you have control of the thermostat. You have the ability to modify the story. You cannot change the actual facts of your past, but you can change the way you view them. For instance, you cannot decide not to have the parents you have. You cannot wash away the broken relationships that gave you a guarded heart. You cannot choose that you were not abused. You cannot fool yourself into thinking that you did not make those bad decisions during your adolescent and young adult years.

You can, however, alter your interpretation of past events. If you had an alcoholic father, you can choose to feel sorry for yourself because you grew up in an unpredictable and disappointing home environment. Or you can choose to recognize that you have insight into the hard reality of life because of your past. You can recognize that you can be strong in the midst of the struggles of life. If you have made a detrimental decision in the past, you have the choice to see yourself either as a failure who cannot make good decisions or a successful person who makes mistakes just like everyone else.

If you have been hurt significantly by someone in your past, you have a number of choices. You can define yourself as a victim who must live in the shadow of a monster who was able to destroy your life. Or you can decide you are a dirty, corrupt individual who deserves to be hurt and misused for the rest of your days. Or you can decide you are an over-

comer who can now make your own decisions. You can choose to not let
the hurts of your past, over which you had no control, determine the
opportunities of your future, over which you *do* have control.

The point is that you have choices. You cannot erase the past, but
you can interpret the past in a way that catapults you into an advanta-
geous position for your future. "Painful stories about our past can stifle
our hope about the future. We need a way of viewing our past story
that does not deny the facts but transforms what the story means for
our future. Forgiveness is the key twist in the plot."[1]

Our lives are a reflection of our view of God. If you have a dim view
of God, you will believe life is a random collection of events that is cru-
elly subject to the whims of people. The inevitable conclusion with this
view is that you are going to be hurt, so you must protect yourself or be
destroyed.

If you believe that God is sovereign in history and able to make all
things right in time, you will look to him for his perspective. You will
seek to view your life the way he does. You will see that every sorrow—not denying its pain—can be turned into an opportunity to help
others. You will believe that "in all things God works for the good of
those who love him" (Rom 8:28). You will recognize that bad things
happen because we live in a broken world, but you will balance that
with God's grace that gives "a crown of beauty instead of ashes, the oil
of gladness instead of mourning, and a garment of praise instead of a
spirit of despair" (Is 61:3).

3. Manage stress in your life. If you are overwhelmed by the responsibilities of your life and you cannot "get away" from the strain of life
emotionally, you will have nothing left for the loving relationships that
make life a joy. Time management, emotional discipline and stress-
relieving activities such as reading, exercise and time with friends are
commitments that must be maintained in a deliberate way if we are to
have any energy left for relationships. We must all ask serious questions of ourselves: What helps me to keep stress at a manageable level
in my life? How often do I need to talk with friends? to read for relax-
ation? to exercise? What are the signs in my life that stress is creeping

up and ready to drag me down?

4. Practice strategic decision-making. Life is filled with obstacles and opportunities that must be navigated wisely. If you have not developed the ability to "get around" in the maze of decisions, you will lack confidence and struggle in your relationships. This is especially true with the decision to get married. Maybe you got married hoping that your spouse would make decisions for you. At first, your spouse will be flattered by the level of trust you appear to exhibit, but over time carrying you through life will become a burden. The end result will be irritation at your lack of initiative and boredom at your lack of genuine contribution to the relationship.

Or maybe you got married because you wanted to control your environment, so you have been trying for years to control your spouse. As a result, your spouse has been passive in the decisions that determine life's outcomes and has not had to take much responsibility in your family. As life gets bigger, your spouse cannot make the strategic decisions that will lead to growth and progress. He or she settles for passive-aggressive behavior, punishing you by inactivity and lack of involvement.

5. Anticipate and prepare for significant events in your life. Birthdays, anniversaries and Valentine's Day are examples of fixed dates in the year that require an extra amount of attention and carry with them additional expectations. If you are unable to "get up" for these days, the pressure in your life goes up and unproductive behavior dominates your relationship. As the special day nears, your irritation level increases. Most people hope that romance and intimate relationships will happen spontaneously and be relatively easy. In reality, these relationships revolve around scheduled events that provide the opportunity to be spontaneous within the boundaries of your calendar. These events give us the privilege in our hectic schedules to focus on the fun part of life. If you can't do this deliberately, these special days become agonizing events of failure.

You may want to try some of these ideas to prepare for these important days.

☐ Ask your spouse for a list of gift ideas. The list should include some dream gifts as well as gifts that could be bought for $10.00 or less.

☐ Talk about the upcoming day about a month before it happens. Ask each other, "What would you like to do this Valentine's Day?" "Do you want to plan our anniversary together or would you like me to plan it this year?" "What are some of the things you would definitely not like to do this year for your birthday?"

☐ Ask your spouse to give you a list of things you could do that would make him or her feel loved. Choose one or two of the things on this list to do on your next special day together. The list might include things like a backrub, making his favorite meal, spending a quiet evening together looking at old photos, drawing a hot bath and giving her time to enjoy it while you put the kids to bed.

Send an invitation for a date you already have planned. Write in the invitation that you are looking forward to the time together.

6. Learn dynamic listening. A key element in communication is being a good listener. We all look for ways to relate to the one we are married to, but because we communicate so differently, we often miscommunicate and irritate one another. Men think women are irrational; women think men are shallow. Neither of these is true, but it can appear that way. What is usually the truth is that we are terrible listeners.

The key to intimate communication is to give permission for your spouse to tell you more. When your spouse wants to talk, try practicing these skills:

☐ Repeat the key phrases spoken by your spouse.

☐ Summarize what your spouse has said in your own words, and ask, "Is that what you are trying to say?"

☐ Try to relate what your spouse is saying to something you have been through. Start with, "This sounds like the time I . . ." Then briefly explain the situation you found yourself in and the way you felt while you were going through this experience. End with the question, "Is that close to what you are trying to explain to me?"

Instead of using these skills, married couples often get defensive and guard their emotional territory so they won't get hurt by one another. This will protect you, but it will also insulate you from each other and guarantee that your relationship will be shallow and dull. If you stay there, it will be impossible to trust one another.

Carl and Ginny had spent a lot of years focused on the struggles in their relationship. Each of them concluded that the problems were the other's fault. As a result, each person patiently but uselessly waited for the other to change. As they learned to trust themselves through focused change, the relationship began to make progress.

Carl explains,

> In my anger against Ginny, I wrote a list of all her faults and all of mine. I thought by writing the list I'd have proof of what a bad wife she'd been. To my surprise the list of my faults was much longer than hers. I held in my hand proof that I needed help! I read in the Bible that God wipes out transgressions, that he doesn't hold them against us. I had a list of transgressions, and I gave that list to God. I accepted his forgiveness.

And Ginny tells her experience:

> Carl had ruined every holiday. He had left on Christmas and Valentine's Day, but he came back home for good on our wedding anniversary in 1983. Even though he was home, it wasn't easy. That fall I was still really struggling with how to forgive Carl. He just didn't seem all that sorry for what he'd done. At a women's retreat, the speaker shared on forgiveness and challenged us to put all our hurts in an imaginary box, place them at the foot of the cross—and leave them there. As I prayed, God reminded me of the verses I had read in John that told how I too was imperfect, and I knew he was asking me to forgive Carl. I placed my pain and hurt in that box and left it with Jesus in prayer. I drove away from that retreat center a free woman. Neither my past nor Carl's was going to hold us back.

Carl sums up the priority of developing strong lives when he says,

> If we think it won't happen to us, we are fools. It can happen to anyone. The mistake most men make is looking for a listening ear and, instead of going to a pastor, Christian counselor or a group of committed Christian guys, they go and cry on the shoulder of another woman—and

then it turns into an affair. Ginny and I now have a new lifetime plan for staying in love. We first had to both grow up and deal with the junk in our own lives so we could enjoy our life together.

Learning to Trust Each Other

Learning to trust God and trust yourself leads to the opportunity to trust each other. This is, of course, the scariest part of the process. In this step, you have to risk. You may trust your spouse and be sorely disappointed, or you may trust and be overwhelmingly fulfilled. That is the nature of a love relationship. There is no way to take the risk out of it. The key is to take calculated risks. The goal here is not to set yourself up for a situation that is guaranteed to hurt, but to take a step toward vulnerability. So what are some of the calculated risks you can take to begin reestablishing intimacy?

Begin dating again. You probably fell in love with each other through some form of courting process. It is in this process that you discover one another's likes, dislikes and values. Courting is a time for exploration and discovery. It is a time for questions and anticipation. Too often, married couples feel that the need to date is over when the wedding is done. But the fact is that we all continue to change and grow. There is a constant exploration and discovery process to be pursued in marriage so that life doesn't grow stale.

When the relationship is in crisis, it is partly because there has been a significant change in each of you that has not been matched by the practice of discovery. You no longer know each other because you haven't kept up with the progress in each other. There is a new you to discover! There is a new person to fall in love with. The person you are married to has a different perspective, different needs and different concerns than were present at the time of your wedding.

You can rediscover one another the same way you first discovered one another. Start dating again. Quiet dinners together will give you opportunity to talk without being interrupted by the responsibilities of life. Walks on the beach or strolls in the park will give you time to talk in a relaxed environment. A trip to the zoo or a night at the theater can create fun memories that add value to the relationship in an enjoyable way. The key to the dating activities is to make them relaxed so you can evaluate your ability to be friends that trust each other.

This has been mentioned before, but we include it again because it needs to be applied in all the contexts of marriage. Dating is an important way to express value to one another. It is vital to staying in touch emotionally. It is one of the keys to restoring trust when the relationship has been violated. There is never a time in marriage when heart-to-heart encounters with genuine communication are optional.

Discuss deliberate questions. Conversation is difficult when there has been a break in trust. As a result, the serious issues you try to explore with one another get interrupted and off track. You may try to discuss the needs of your kids but end up pointing out the deficiencies in each other's parenting style. Your attempt to discuss finances may turn into accusations of how his family has always been intrusive in your relationship, thus making him irresponsible. This is especially frustrating for the spouse who is less skilled with words. He will feel intimidated and overwhelmed by her ability to flow freely in conversation. She will feel simple-minded or inadequate because of his vocabulary or seemingly impeccable logic.

In order to avoid the tangled web of conversation that often happens in the midst of reconciliation efforts, make a list of the questions you would like to discuss with your spouse. Schedule times to talk, focusing on this list. Discuss the questions one at a time. There is no rush to get through the list. The goal here is to develop a track record of honest discussion that is backed up by action in life. As you discuss one issue at a time, there will be dialogue back and forth. It will result in a conclusion of some sort. Life's experience will prove whether this conclusion is heartfelt or just conversation. If action backs up the conversation, trust will start to develop. If action does not support the conversation, then trust will be threatened. But at least you will know!

Trust requires a track record. No single event can convince you that your spouse is now someone you can put faith in. You need a number of trust-building events to make you feel secure that the past is behind you and the future is going to be good. The goal, therefore, is not to rush through the list of concerns and questions. The goal is to create specific opportunities to build trust. If trust is established in a firm and believable way, the rest of the list will probably lose its intensity. You will still need to discuss the list, but the issues will be areas of cooperation rather than tests of trust.

Carl commented on the need he and Ginny had to reearn one another's trust through a series of successes.

> But trust didn't spring back overnight. I knew I had to reearn Ginny's trust. I decided to invite her wherever I went—business trips, Home Depot, the grocery store. If she didn't want to go, fine, but I wasn't going to have unaccounted-for time in her eyes.

Ginny added,

> That helped. Reading the Bible together and praying every day helped. Knowing Carl was in a men's Bible study accountability group helped. But what helped most was one day when we were driving in the car together and a radio show came on about the effects of affairs on a family. It got very quiet in the car. Then I saw a tear roll down Carl's cheek and he said, "Ginny, I am so sorry for the hurt I caused you and the kids." He said he was willing to do anything to reearn a relationship with us.

"I needed to reverbalize my love and commitment for Ginny," Carl added. "I took her to a favorite spot in the mountains and we renewed our wedding vows together. Ginny wasn't sure if I meant it at the time, but I did."

"He did," related Ginny with excitement in her voice. "Every day he is a servant to me, the kids and the church. He is leading our men's ministry so other men can learn from his mistakes."

Receive training together. The patterns the two of you have developed as a couple have given you the relationship you have today. In order to have a better relationship you must develop new patterns of interaction. This will happen only if you get outside information. You cannot work harder at things that are not working and expect them to help!

There are a number of ways to get new information to integrate into your relationship:

1. Read a book together. There are a lot of good books on marriage that discuss the distinct struggles you may be encountering. Reading these books together should create new levels of discussion between the two of you. Our books *Pure Pleasure: Making Your Marriage a Great Affair, Love to Love You* and *Marriage in the Whirlwind* are written to help you. *Traits of a Lasting Marriage* by Jim and Sally Conway is filled with wise, practical advice. We have also found the writings of James Dobson, Gary Smalley, and Les and Leslie Parrott to be very helpful to couples.

2. Attend a marriage conference. They are great resources for gaining new information. You get away from the pressures of your everyday life and think together about your relationship. You will spend more quality time together on a weekend getaway than you probably will in the next four months of everyday life. In addition, you will be hearing proven ideas for making your relationship successful.

3. Attend a few sessions with a counselor or pastor. Individual counseling can be a great boost to your relationship because it is focused on you as a couple. It gives you a chance to do hands-on practice that is designed for where you are as a couple, with coaching from a trained professional. It is good to ask around and research who is skilled at giving training in marriage issues. Each professional has an area of expertise, and not all counselors are adept at helping married couples. Look for someone who has the knowledge to hone your skills as a couple.

When you increase your skills as a couple you also increase your confidence as a couple. When you increase your ability to communicate, you gain a sense of security with one another. When you grow in your ability to manage your life together, the stress level in your home goes down. When you learn to appreciate the differences between you as a man and woman, the level of passion in your relationship becomes stronger and more mature. But change will take time. Once you rebuild trust you will be glad you took the time to do it, but the process can seem long and drawn out.

Guidelines for Choosing a Mentor Couple

1. Find a couple who has accomplished the things in life you would like to accomplish.

2. Find a couple who has the kind of relationship you would like to have when you get to be their age.

3. Find a couple who has a track record of influencing others, so that you can have confidence they will be interested in influencing you.

4. Ask them to mentor you. It is best to set up an appointment to talk with them. Don't leave this step up to chance, and don't ask them in passing.

5. Tell them what you need from them and what they can expect from you. Address questions such as, How often will you meet? Who will set the agenda for the meetings? Will you go through a written curriculum, or do you want to keep it casual? What subjects do you want to address? How long do you want this couple to commit to being mentors? How long will you meet each time?

6. Don't expect them to work too hard at helping you. You should plan on doing any research that is needed to facilitate your conversations. You should take responsibility for scheduling your get-togethers, reminding them when appropriate and communicating about any changes.

Carl exclaimed,

> Time. That was exactly what I needed. I needed time. Time to decide what I was going to do. I grabbed the Bible on impulse on my way out the door. In my room that night I decided I would see what this Bible had to say. I didn't know much about it. I expected to find a whole lot of stories about perfect people. I wasn't sure where to start, so I decided that since I have a son named David, and I knew that name was in the Bible, I would read about David's life. As I read about David, I realized I was reading about myself. A man at the top of his world who had an affair and saw his world crumbling around his feet. As I read about David and saw that God had a plan for him, I realized that maybe God had a plan for me too.

And Ginny summarized confidently,

> I wouldn't trade anything for what I have now. Seeing Carl with the
> grandkids, sharing our lives together, even going for silent rides in the
> car, it is heaven now. I'm glad I gave God time to intervene.

Focus on the Heart

*Lord, teach me to trust. Teach me to trust you as the giver of life. Teach me to
trust myself as one who is created in your image. And teach me to trust my spouse
as a gift from your hand.*

A Step Toward Love

Watching another couple in action can do a lot to help you learn to
rebuild trust. Begin looking for a couple or couples who could be good
role models for you and your spouse to emulate.

Nine

Restoring Passion

I*t was dark that night as I (Pam) pulled out of the church parking lot.* Walking slowly along was a young woman with her four tiny children in tow. She had visited our church that night. I pulled up next to her.

"Excuse me, Trish. Can I give you and your kids a ride home? It's so dark, I'd feel much better if you'd let me give you all a ride home."

"Sure!" She smiled, then opened the car door, piled her kids in the back and buckled them in.

As Trish got in the car, her story tumbled out. She was unhappy, living with a boyfriend, wanting to know more about God. We set up an appointment for later in the week. At that appointment, I learned that Trish had been sexually abused by a member of her own family. She had looked for love in the arms of the boys at her high school, and at sixteen she had found herself pregnant and not married. She wasn't sure what to do, so she married the guy who had fathered her child. He took her up into the mountains outside San Diego.

He would leave her and the baby—and soon two babies—alone for days while he went and did his own thing. He left her without any heat, electricity, food, diapers, money or transportation. He had them living in a small travel trailer. Things got so bad that Trish had to ask the farmers in the area if she could glean their fields in order to get food for her children. This all took place in the 1980s in southern California.

One day a high-school friend of her husband stopped by to visit. Of course her husband was gone. Jeff, the friend, saw how Trish was living and said, "Trish, you can't live this way! Why don't you and the kids come live with me."

Trish thought she'd found her knight in shining armor! She left her husband and moved in with Jeff, hoping to live happily ever after.

But it was no storybook life. Soon Jeff began to take her welfare check and spend it on drugs, alcohol and gifts for other women. He even brought home a sexually transmitted disease. Conflicts heightened until Trish found herself in a physically abusive relationship with Jeff. That's when I met Trish.

One day, sitting in the park while our children played I said, "Trish, God really loves you and he has a wonderful plan for your life, but this isn't it."

"I know." Trish responded anxiously, "I know this isn't good for the kids. I know it's especially not good for my daughter to see. I don't want her to grow up and have this kind of life. And I don't want the boys to grow up and be this kind of guy—but what do I do?"

I explained that God would want her to courageously move out of the live-in relationship and take the kids to a safe place. Then God could help her rebuild her life. We discussed some options for surviving this situation. We also talked about people at church that would walk alongside her through the transition. Finally, we helped Trish move out.

Jeff stormed into my (Bill) office. "Who do you think you are? Don't you know that I'm the best thing that ever happened to Trish!"

I calmly explained that Jeff wasn't the best thing that ever happened to Trish. He had taken her money and her self-respect. In addition, he'd hurt her physically and emotionally. Jeff marched out and slammed the door behind him. We never thought we'd see Jeff again.

A few months later, Jeff marched back into my office, sat on the sofa and announced, "OK, Pastor, we'll do it God's way!"

Obviously God had been working on Jeff. Trish had contacted Jeff after many months of silence. She had communicated to Jeff that, even though it wasn't healthy for her and the kids to be living with him right now, God loved Jeff. She said that she was concerned for Jeff because of his rowdy lifestyle. Jeff was in church that Sunday and then in my office that week.

Jeff's story tumbled out in his encounter with me. Jeff had been raised by parents who were actively involved in the sexual revolution. His parents had actively participated in spouse-swapping parties. Jeff had even walked in on some of their sexual experiments while he was a child. When Jeff was thirteen, his dad sat him down with a stack of pornography and said, "Jeff, it's time for you to become a man." Then he gave him a tour through the pages of *Playboy, Penthouse* and other forms of pornography much more graphic than these popular magazines.

Jeff said to me, "You say that I can be happy and sexually satisfied with one woman, but I've had sex with over forty women. I lost count after that. And you are saying one woman, in marriage for a lifetime, will satisfy?"

"Exactly," I replied enthusiastically.

"I don't believe it!" exclaimed Jeff. "I want to, but that seems impossible."

So what does a person say to two people who are so wounded sexually?

Get a New Start

Pam rigorously walked Trish through the steps of forgiveness for all the people that had hurt her. At the same time, Bill walked Jeff through forgiveness steps for all the people that had hurt him. They were both amazed at how deep the need for forgiveness ran in their lives.

It was obvious that Trish needed to forgive her first husband, but she was surprised at the frustration with her parents that surfaced. She reasoned that if her parents had better prepared her for adulthood she probably never would have committed herself to a bad relationship. She was determined not to pass on the same naiveté to her children, but she wanted to do it with good motives. Living in reaction to what her parents didn't do wasn't enough to make a lasting change.

She then had to come to grips with the reality that her decisions were her decisions. Her parents had influenced her, but she had chosen to become sexually active during high school. She had chosen to marry an irresponsible man. She had decided to have her children live in sub-par conditions. Forgiving herself for all this launched her into a yo-yo experience that bounced her from guilt to relief and back again.

"Who am I to say that anybody else is wrong when I have done all these things?" Trish said early in the process. "I feel like such a hypocrite, and yet I can't continue living like this."

She didn't always feel like forgiving herself, but she was determined to finish the process for her sake and the quality of her children's future. Gradually she saw the healing process take hold in her heart. Her confidence was growing steadily, her self-respect was blossoming and her convictions were taking firm shape. She even surprised herself when she realized she needed to forgive Jeff for the sexual activities he had been involved in with her and with others. She had previously dismissed these as issues of the past that should not be resurrected, but as she grew she realized that those activities were the outgrowth of unhealthy patterns in Jeff's life that had now affected her and her children.

Having dealt with her disappointment with her parents, Trish gained the confidence to confront Jeff's abusive treatment. Previously, Jeff had seemed too strong for her to ever oppose. She didn't even dare evaluate him honestly. Now she was able to see that Jeff was just as wounded as she was and needed the same healing. So that her attitudes would not get in the way of God's work in his life, she let go of her own anger and put him firmly in God's hands.

Jeff's journey was remarkably similar. He discovered an anger with his parents that he had buried under a mountain of self-destructive behavior. He had pursued drinking and sexual encounters in an attempt to hide from the reality of his home life. He had finally reached a point where he was tired of running, and so he turned around and faced the situation. He forgave his parents for their selfish lifestyle and for exposing him to the world of sex before he was mature enough to handle it.

Having cleared that hurdle, he then forgave himself for buying into the influence. Now that he was old enough to take a sober look at his life, he wished he had made different choices. He didn't have the same struggle with guilt that Trish did, but he too was surprised by the depth of his need to forgive Trish for the choices she had made. He was angry about her first marriage and the conditions she put her kids in. He was impatient with her naiveté. Even though he was not a part of those decisions, his heart was strangely tied to her entire history. As he walked through the six-month-long process of forgiving, he too found a new level of confidence in his life. Having faced the truth of his past with honesty seemed to give him the ability to deliberately choose the future he wanted.

Through this process, Jeff and Trish each made strong personal commitments to Jesus. They realized they had not done very well on their own, so they asked God to forgive them. And they intensely relied on God's strength and the principles of the Bible to lead them as individuals.

They got together casually and shared their stories with each other. The remarkable similarities in their experience of forgiveness began to develop a new bond between them. As they continued to talk, they thought that maybe God was calling them back into a dating relationship. As a safeguard against repeating their past performances, they started with relationship counseling. The process of discovering the new possibilities that were open to them strengthened their new attachment to one another. Pre-engagement counseling followed. During this process they each wrote lists, discussed them, and asked for and gave forgiveness. Finally, they participated in engagement counseling that helped build healthy relationship skills into their lives. They spent time getting to know married couples who were stable and growing, and they each sought out healthy role models.

Bill performed the wedding where Jeff and Trish pledged their love to one another. Pam was the matron of honor. Trish's children were all a part of the ceremony as Jeff and Trish not only committed themselves to each other but spoke vows they had written that included promises to the children.

That was many years ago. Jeff and Trish have gone on to have several children together and are serving God in youth ministry.

Seeking Sexual Intimacy
Sexual intimacy is one of the strangest and yet most satisfying experiences of human existence. We all have the sense that sex is supposed to be an event that brings a couple incredibly close and cements them together as partners. The act of sexual intimacy includes the joining of two bodies, so that for a short period of time the two move as one and are totally lost in each other. This is a powerful and highly intense aspect of human interaction. In a good sexual relationship, the level of intimacy and cooperation is astounding. There is unity. And there is a security that makes us feel almost invincible.

Because of the intense nature of sexual interaction, it becomes a veritable battleground for couples in crisis. As a background for our discussion about restoring passion, let's talk about the differences in the way men and women approach the sexual dimension of marriage.

Men Are Like Waffles
The basic difference between a man and a woman, other than the obvious physical uniqueness, can be summed up in the phrase, "Men are like waffles; women are like spaghetti."

If you were to diagram the way a man thinks about life, it would look like a waffle: a number of boxes all separated from each other by walls. A man will take an issue of life and place it in its own box. The next issue goes in the next box, and so on. Men, then, tend to live in one box at a time.

When a man is at work, he is at work. When a man is exercising, he is exercising. When a man is working in the garage, he is focused on the project at hand. When a man is making love with his wife, he is focused on the sexual box and is not thinking about anything else in life. That is why men can become interested in sex so quickly.

A husband will be going about his routine at home and catch a glimpse of his wife changing her clothes. He is transported in his mind to the sex box and is suddenly interested in being romantic with her. She is shocked. She can't figure out where the interest came from, since they haven't talked for a while.

Many will say that the sex box must be the biggest box in a man's waffle, because it seems that is all he ever thinks about. The reason it looks that way is that a man's sexual needs are different from any other needs in his life. There is a constant buildup of semen in a man's body that longs to be released, and there is a constant infusion of testosterone that drives a man to think about sexual activities.

For a man to keep this in balance in his life requires a mature level of discipline. If a man fails to discipline this drive in his life, he may become aggressive and demanding, and that can easily lead to abusive behavior. He can turn into a man on the hunt who is driven by the possibility of victory and the thrill of conquest. This drive can turn into involvement with pornography or deviant behavior that is both unhealthy and detrimental.

When a married couple is not sexually active because of conflict or mistrust, the husband becomes irritable and agitated. He may be aware that he has done little to arouse his wife's interest, but he can't turn off his desire. He may become consumed with the idea of sex but be embarrassed to admit it. He feels he should have more self-control, yet he realizes he cannot master it. He feels he should be more mature than to let his thoughts run to sex so much, yet the physiological drive is enormous. His wife's physical needs regarding sex are so very different that she cannot empathize.

The man may be afraid to let his wife know just how much power she has over his well-being. If she was ever to tune in to his need for intercourse, she could get him to do anything she wants. He knows this is true but fears that if he admits it to his wife, she will use it to take advantage of him. Yet he longs to have his wife understand. He lives with this paradox in his heart. And he is frustrated by the sense that she never really will know—and he will never really know how to explain it to her.

I (Bill) was talking with a couple in my office one day, and this topic came up. The wife was feeling taken for granted because her husband seemed more interested in having sex with her than in talking with her. She loved him but was having trouble being sexually responsive to him. She longed for him to communicate with her, but the only time he seemed interested in her as a person was when he wanted sex. As I tried to lead the husband in a discussion with his wife about what it was like to have a male sex drive, it was obvious that he was not going to succeed in explaining the paradox to his wife. So I jumped in.

"When a man hasn't had sex for a while, he feels a driving urge in his body that becomes all-consuming. He tries to think of other things, but everything appears sexual to him. His wife becomes more attractive, and all other activities seem insignificant. The whole time he is telling himself, 'Come on, big guy, get a hold of yourself. There are other things you need to be doing. She's not in the mood and, even if she was, you are being a real klutz about this. Why would she be interested in having sex right now anyway? But she has to be willing, because I can't focus on anything else until we do.'

"When his advances are rejected there is an almost instant response of frustration and anger. He isn't really mad at his wife. He is just mad. He has this drive that is screaming to be met, and he doesn't know how to divert it. There is a certain desperation associated with the sex drive that takes on a life of its own. Once a man ejaculates, the world changes. He is suddenly relaxed and more reasonable. The colors are brighter; everyone seems nicer. Little things are now interesting because life has returned to normal."

As the wife sat spellbound, her husband was enthusiastically nodding his head up and down. She had never had anyone explain to her how a man deals with his sex drive, and he had never been able to make any progress in helping her understand his struggle. This one conversation did not resolve their struggle, but it began a new series of conversations about the different ways the two of them approach life.

Women Are Like Spaghetti

Women, on the other hand, approach life more like a plate of spaghetti. Everything is connected to everything else. If you try to follow one noodle around the plate, you will switch to another noodle without even being aware that you have changed. If you can imagine that each noodle represents an issue in a woman's life, then you get insight into how a woman thinks through life. Every issue is connected to every other issue. She will journey around her life seamlessly switching from one idea to another. In conversation, she will change subjects at will and never become disconnected in her thoughts. In her planning, she will think about her career goals, quickly switch to the kids' needs and then jump to her vacation plans. For her husband this is frustrating— he is frantically jumping boxes trying to keep up with her.

In the sexual arena this has a profound impact. For the wife, sexual interaction with her husband is connected to everything else in her life. Her career, her relationship with her children, the quality and quantity of her interaction with her husband and the condition of her house will affect her sexual responsiveness. Romantic getaways are very helpful because they shrink her world and give her less things to have to coordinate. Her whole world, for the time being, can be limited to the romantic surroundings and her relationship with her husband. In this setting, sexual intimacy is easier.

Coordinating Sexual Needs

While men tend to keep everything separate, their wives want to connect everything in life. Men sit impatiently wanting to release the sexual tension in their bodies, while their wives are wanting to talk and experience a closeness that will bring all things into focus in their relationship.

Although this difference can be frustrating, a couple who harnesses the diversity of their sexual energy will experience satisfying sexual lives with an enjoyable amount of variety. Couples who don't embrace the differences find sexual activity to be emotionally painful. This person who used to be so attractive and fulfilling to be around is now unattractive and demanding. The respect is gone, and joy has been replaced with expectations.

Many couples resort to putting pressure on each other to change. Wives expect husbands to be more like women, developing verbal and nurturing skills equal to their own. Husbands expect their wives to be more like men, learning to become more adventurous and spontaneous in their sexual advances. When couples resort to this behavior, it is about as appetizing as putting pancake syrup on spaghetti and marinara sauce on waffles.

Coordinating sexual needs is a challenge even for couples who are doing well. When a couple has been in crisis, it is even more difficult and agonizing. When a couple is in crisis, either the partners will avoid sexual activity or one partner will take advantage of the weakened condition of the other. A married couple who is not sexually active will always be in conflict because the sexual tension will be too high. Some couples will fight tenaciously, while others will avoid one another, dreading the pain of rejection. A partner who is having sex without developing emotional intimacy will soon feel used and will resent the relationship.

Trust Fuels Passion

In order for a couple to recapture the passion of sexual love, trust must be vigorously developed. Successful sexual relationships are an extension of vulnerable interaction. Without trust individuals will not willingly expose themselves. So how does a couple with a fractured relationship get started with the process of rebuilding the kind of trust that encourages sexual passion? Here are some steps you can take.

1. Pray together often. Offering yourself sexually will be a huge challenge after you have been hurt. To do so effectively you will need to be convinced that honest change has taken place in the heart of your spouse. If you think your spouse might betray you again, you are unlikely to willingly participate in sexual activity. On the other hand, if you believe your spouse has genuinely changed, hope can be rekindled. If you become convinced the change is permanent, you may even discover a new level of passion that didn't exist before the crisis you have been through.

When a couple prays, they give each other insight into the way their hearts beat. It is difficult to be insincere in prayer. Many people struggle with praying out loud because it instantly makes them vulnerable.

When a wife hears her husband pray, she sees the soft and caring side of his nature. She gains insight into the compassion and love for people he possesses but is reluctant to display in the midst of the daily responsibilities of life.

When a husband hears his wife pray, he sees the consistency of her love for people and for life. In the daily grind of life, especially after a crisis in marriage, a woman needs consistent input that says she is secure and desired by her husband. She will ask lots of questions, long for conversation and test the strength of her relationship on a regular basis. A husband can get worn out by this consistent need in his wife's life. In prayer, the tests are set aside as she melts into the security of a relationship with Christ. Her prayer cuts through her needs and reveals her heart. As he sees the strength of her passion for God, her husband may be more willing to trust her and meet her needs.

2. Deliberately romance one another. Romance is an active attempt to show that your thoughts are centered on another individual. The actual activity is not as important as the fact that you thought about your spouse with enough respect and attention to consider what would be pleasing to him or her. When a husband takes the time to set up a night that is focused on the actual needs of his wife, she gets the message—in a tangible way—that he thinks she is important. Words are helpful, but at the conclusion of a crisis, words can ring hollow. Sacrificial actions focused on the desires of his wife will make a husband's words more believable.

When a wife goes out of her way to set up a date she knows her husband will enjoy, he gets the impression that there is hope. His sense of inadequacy as a lover and conversationalist starts to give way to the confidence that he can meet her needs. Her selfless actions tells him that she cares about his needs and that she wants to have a workable relationship. He concludes that he will not be punished his whole life for the mistakes he has made with her. Romance is not a magic wand that insures sexual unity, but it helps break down the walls in a couple's ability to be vulnerable with each other.

3. Verbally voice your commitment. One of the main reasons couples do not reinitiate sexual activity quickly after reconciliation is that they are afraid the relationship may not last. It is threatening to give yourself in a sexual way to someone who does not cherish the relationship and who is not committed to seeing it through the ups and downs. A mutually satisfying sexual relationship develops best in an environment of commitment. It is easy to have awkward moments when you interact sexually, and often the only thing that heals the wounds of these clumsy adventures is the security that there will be other times to experiment and reestablish a sense of unity and love.

In a time of crisis the need to voice your commitment is only intensified. If a break in trust has occurred, the fear of rejection will hang around the couple like an unwelcome house guest.

You try to draw close to one another, and rejection says, "Be careful. Remember what she did."

You apologize, and the uninvited guest interjects, "He is just tired of not having sex. You can't trust him."

You plan a special weekend together to get reacquainted, and the incessant intruder argues, "This is useless. There has been too much hurt."

You must win the argument by combating the influence of rejection with the cover of commitment. It won't happen quickly, but each time you voice your commitment, the volume goes down on the fear of rejection. Your words will be tested and challenged and ignored, but they are still working. The bigger the hurt, the more influence the fear has and the longer it will take for your announcements of dedication to win over your loved one.

It is good to decide ahead of time the words that best express the strength of your commitment, because this vessel will be sailing on stormy seas. You will be told you don't really mean it, that you are just saying what you have to say, that you are desperate. If your words are fragile, they will be drowned out by the waves of denial. As a result, you need to choose phrases ahead of time and practice them often until the seas calm down.

You may want to choose or modify one or more of the following statements to express your commitment to your spouse. "I know we have made mistakes in the past, but I am committed to you for the rest of my life." "I am here. I am not just saying that we will be miserable together for the rest of our lives. I am committing myself to build a growing relationship with you." "It doesn't matter if I get hurt—I am not going to give up on us." "I am willing to work through whatever challenges get thrown at us." "I love you and, no matter how hard it is to rebuild our relationship, I am going to give it my all."

4. Be sensitive. Many of your encounters will not work out. There will be times when you will decide together to share a sexual experience but it will not go well. One or the other of you may get triggered by some emotion that interrupts your ability to carry through with your desire. This is to be expected because of the intensity of the vulnerability necessary to share intimate sexual interaction. Another possibility is that one of you may just go numb. If this happens, there will not be an honest relationship. One of you will be operating behind a wall of false pretenses. It is better to be honest with one another and share the awkward reality of fumbled experiences than to live a lie with one another.

The key is to be sensitive to the inevitable failure of some of your sexual events. When you get your hopes up but your spouse is unable to follow through, use the episode to express your love and the desire you have to be close for the rest of your life, not just tonight. You will feel like getting angry and will be tempted to think it will never work, but don't give up. The fact that your spouse has tried is evidence of interest in you. If you foster the interest rather than point out the failure, the most recent frustration could be the catalyst that will cause your love to grow.

5. Talk about your sexual interaction. As previously stated, the basis of a good sexual relationship is trust, and the road to trust is paved with vulnerable conversation. As trust grows, your willingness to talk about the progress of your sexual encounters with each other will encourage further vulnerability in your relationship. Don't just talk about your successes! Explore the issues involved with the encounters that fell apart, and see what you can learn. Ask questions like, "What went wrong?" "Could we have avoided the awkwardness of our last time together?" "Thanks for trying the other night—are you doing all right?"

Don't expect to solve the problem as much as simply to explore the new dynamic of your sexual relationship. The sexual expression of love is capable of incredibly intense experiences as well as incredibly ridiculous encounters. Trying to figure them out or solve them is the wrong tactic. Sex is to be enjoyed and explored but never to be controlled. Therefore, as a couple explores their feelings and thoughts about their sexual life, they enter into a world of fascination that draws them together with an intimacy they share with no one else.

6. Be patient. Marriage relationships take time to change. If your relationship was harmed by the actions of your spouse, you have probably realized it was the culmination of years of mistrust and miscommunication. In the same way, it will take a while to restore your relationship to the level of intimacy you both desire. The process will be prolonged because you cannot go back to the relationship you had—that one didn't work! You must build a whole new relationship with different communication patterns, different boundaries and a different level of respect for yourselves and each other.

In time, you will discover that you have a much greater ability to forgive than you thought you had. You will realize that you can face much bigger challenges than you thought. You will find out that you have the strength of the heroes you have read about, but it has been dormant because you didn't need to tap the depths of the strength in your life. As you grasp the truth that you are an incredibly strong individual and that you are married to someone strong enough to endure the dark hours of life with you, you will recognize that your relationship is much stronger than you previously thought.

Sex Has Never Been Better

A few year ago, Trish and I (Pam) were visiting while sitting on a front porch swing. I asked Trish if she was happy.

"Yes," Trish smiled confidently. "I used to have sex just to make sure Jeff came home to me each night, but now I rest in his love."

About the same time, Jeff and I (Bill) were visiting in our front yard.

"You know, Bill, I thought you were crazy when you said that I could have sex with just one woman and be happy. Man, you're right! It's been years now, and my sex life with just Trish is great—in fact, sex has never been better."

Focus on the Heart

God of love, give me a deep love for my spouse. Give me a marriage that is characterized by passion and support rather than pain and conflict. Reignite my passion for the partner of my life.

A Step Toward Love

Go on a date this week. In preparation for your time together think about the statement, "Men are like waffles; women are like spaghetti." Each of you make a list of the ways this statement applies to your spouse and how each item on the list improves your life together. Share your lists with each other on your date.

Ten

I'm the Only One
Who Wants to Work
on the Relationship

Y*ou may be saying at this point, "It is useless for me to work through the* process of forgiveness because my spouse will never join me. I am the only one who wants to work on this relationship." If this is you, do not give up hope. Even one person can make a difference.

If you are willing to master forgiveness and make it operative in your life, you will empower yourself. This puts you in a good place because everything in life works in systems. Every act affects every other act, and every decision influences every other decision. Therefore, if forgiveness frees you up to change the way you do things, it will by necessity cause change in the lives of those you are closest to. Your growth will inspire change in your children, your closest friends and your spouse—even if you are not focused on changing them!

Every Action Brings a Reaction
The dynamic of your relationship is the culmination of interactions between you and your spouse. Conversations are the interaction of

verbal reactions. Your values are the result of the interaction of your desires.

Susan grew up in a home where her father was unpredictable. He had grown up with a father who was harsh and unyielding. He felt he could never live up to his father's expectations, and he responded by becoming a hard-working, hard-driving businessman. This drive provided well for his family but made his relationships unworkable. Susan learned early in life that her father would never be fully pleased with her behavior or accomplishments. As a result, she hung around underachievers in high school because they were easy to be around. Their expectations were low, and their acceptance level was high. She thought she had found the perfect life with people who were just like her.

After high school she met Brian. She was attracted to him by his easygoing, carefree manner. He would laugh easily and had a simple life with few complications. He seemed to always have time to talk and listen to her concerns. They spent long hours walking on the beach and swinging at the park.

The first two years of their marriage went well, with only minor irritations. Susan liked it because Brian allowed her to be in charge. Brian liked it because Susan kept their life organized and smooth-running. Brian could relax very easily, and Susan could feel secure as she took care of Brian and their home.

Everything changed when they had children. Susan wanted to keep working because she loved her job, but Brian did not want to help with the child-care responsibilities. Brian also peaked in his desire to provide for the family. He felt like he was working hard enough and that the gap between what he made and what the family needed was Susan's responsibility to manage. Susan was becoming fatigued and frustrated as her schedule filled up. She worked all day, helped the kids with homework, did housework and coordinated the kids' increasingly active schedules. While she was speeding up, Brian was winding down. He went to work daily but spent most nights either watching television or tinkering in the garage. He refused to help with the domestic or nurturing needs of their family.

Aggressive Ineffectiveness

Susan spent a couple of years yelling and stomping around the house. She often confronted Brian verbally with her desire to have him more involved with the family. Most of these discussions turned into heated arguments after which Brian would generally leave the house in disgust, accusing Susan of being unreasonable and irrational. The net result of these conversations was no change, except that Susan was becoming increasingly bitter about being responsible for the family while Brian continued to watch television.

Susan was putting plenty of effort into trying to change the relationship but was getting nowhere. If she was to have any hope of making a difference, she was going to have to shift her focus from what Brian *wasn't* doing to what she *could* do to help the situation. The bitterness would have to surrender to forgiveness. In her frustration she began asking questions of trusted friends who pointed out to her that she was actually encouraging Brian to be irresponsible. Her willingness to work full-time while also handling all household chores was giving him the freedom not to help. Her commitment to meeting all of her kids' needs was letting him off the hook. Her emotional appeals to Brian were providing an opportunity for him to discredit her and ignore the substance of her concerns. The loser in all these situations was Susan. She was the one getting tired. She was the one carrying the stress of the family. She was the one everyone was disappointed in when something didn't work out.

In talking with these friends over the course of a few months, she got a clear view of how she could make real changes in her relationship with Brian. If she wanted Brian to take on more responsibility, she would have to strategically choose which responsibilities she would no longer fulfill. If she wanted Brian to be a more active father, she would have to decide which of the kids' needs she would let go unfulfilled until Brian stepped up. If she wanted Brian to be a better provider and take on more financial responsibility, she would need to rearrange her financial needs so she could work less, or she would have to decide which bills she would be responsible for and take care of. And she would have to stand firm!

The choices were now clear to Susan. She could see how her actions were allowing Brian to be irresponsible. She could even see how she had learned this pattern from her relationship with her father. But the steps that would make real change were too hard for her—she felt like the cost was too high. All she could see was that her kids would have to pay the price if she changed. They would miss out on activities and friendships. They would experience an increased level of stress, so she concluded it was better for her to suffer than for her children to be inconvenienced.

Making Real Changes

The turning point for Susan came the day her son blew up at her. She had been caught in traffic on her way home from work. Her son was supposed to be at baseball practice at 5:30, but she didn't arrive home until 6:15. When she walked in the door, her son unloaded on her.

"Mom, why weren't you here? You're always letting me down. Everything else is more important to you than my needs!"

"Hey, calm down," she said.

"I don't want to calm down. You're so busy that I miss out on the things the rest of my friends get to enjoy. I hate this!" At that he stormed up the stairs and slammed the door to his bedroom.

Susan was standing at the bottom of the stairs in stunned silence when Brian walked up and said, "What was that all about?"

She spun around and glared at him in shocked surprise.

"How long have you been home?" she blurted out.

"Oh, I got home early today—around 4:00."

"Why didn't you take Justin to practice? You've been home for two hours and you couldn't even give your son a ride?"

"Hey, look. I work hard, and I was tired. I needed the time to rest. Besides, it's your job to get the kids to their activities."

Susan's blood began to boil. She realized her friends were right. She had her whole family trained to dump on her. She was working harder than any of them, yet she was still the focus of their disapproval. When she realized she was disappointing them while working so hard, she decided she would instead disappoint them by cutting back on some of her responsibilities. Then the rest of her family would have to decide what was really important to them. Brian would have to decide if he wanted his kids to have any advantages. The kids would have to prioritize their activities and treat her with more respect.

The first couple of months under this new plan were very stressful. The kids complained about having to rely on Dad for rides because he often refused to oblige. The family voiced their frustration at having to eat out more often because Susan refused to make dinner every night and Brian wasn't about to fill in the gap. Everybody moaned about the pile of clean clothes that were now put on each person's bed rather than put away in the closets. Susan was determined, however. She was very disappointed in Brian and even despised her dad for creating the struggle initially, but she was determined to disarm the pain with forgiveness. She stuck to the conviction that she needed to do only *her* part in the family, not everybody else's as well.

Eventually things began to change. Brian got tired of hearing the kids complain about not getting to activities on time, so he started driving them. The kids started asking Dad to get more involved as they realized Mom would not do everything. Everybody dropped some of the activities they were doing, and they simplified the family schedule. As a result, Susan had time to sit with Brian and talk. As they spent a couple of nights a week visiting, she began to remember what it was about Brian that had attracted her in the first place. She still lived with the nagging sense that she now wasn't doing enough for the family, but that was better than the pain she had felt when everyone was leaning too heavily on her.

By establishing priorities and limiting her responsibilities in life, Susan was able to get her whole family to change. She never directly told her family members what they needed to do to change. She simply told them what she was going to do—and not do. Because all families operate in systems, the actions of any one member of the family cause change in every other member. But this kind of change is accessible only to those who tenaciously forgive. Bitterness robs us of motivation to forgive by intensifying focus on the pain and convincing us that our options are limited.

Every Decision Inspires Other Decisions

Just as actions produce reactions, decisions on your part will lead to decisions on the part of your spouse. Because of this, you are never powerless to make changes in your relationship, even if you are the only one willing.

One common decision that many individuals make is the decision to operate like a healthy partner even if the relationship is not healthy. In a healthy relationship, a husband and wife will encourage one another with kind words, go out of their way to make life more workable and find ways to make one another feel valued. A husband in a disappointing relationship may decide to start complimenting his wife on a regular basis—not because she particularly deserves it but because it is the healthy thing to do. Or a wife may decide to start thanking her husband for the things he does for the family—even if it is a small list! He may wonder what is going on and why she is being so nice; she can respond that she is doing what any healthy wife would do. When one of you starts to make healthy decisions, it gets the attention of the other and subtly encourages everyone in the home to make healthier decisions.

Reverend Scott Wooddell of Fort Worth, Texas, shared the secret of giving positive feedback when he wrote the following to "Dear Abby":

> I am a pastor and have been involved in marital and premarital counseling. My experience has taught me that happiness and passion in marriage do not come from finding the "right" partner, but in being the right partner.
>
> I once heard about a woman who was unhappy in her marriage and angry at her husband. When she went to her lawyer to begin divorce proceedings, she asked his advice on what she could do to really hurt

her lousy husband. The lawyer thought for a moment and suggested that for the next couple of months she love him and romance him with every ounce of her being—and then, once he was happy and fulfilled, she serve him with the divorce papers. "It will rip his heart out," the lawyer promised.

The woman followed his advice. Several months later, she returned to the lawyer's office. He handed her the divorce papers to examine before serving them to her husband, and the woman replied, "I won't be needing them now. We're getting ready to leave on our second honeymoon."[1]

Decide to Keep Growing Up

Another important factor is a commitment to personal growth. Unhealthy relationships develop because of a lack of growth on the part of the individuals involved. Just like anything in life that is neglected, the marriage will deteriorate and stagnate. The pressures and responsibilities of life will become bigger than the couple's ability to keep up with them, and the relationship will either drift into a rut or get caught up in a storm of crisis and confrontation. If just one of you decides to undertake the process of growing, you will increase your skill level at approaching life and will indirectly encourage your spouse to grow to keep up with you. Even if your spouse does not respond to the same level you are growing to, your skills will have increased in responding to the gaps your spouse leaves in life.

Early in her thirties, Pam went through what I (Bill) now affectionately call "The Awakening." We had talked about her going back to college to finish her degree and had set a date of approximately three years in the future. One day, Pam woke up and felt an intense need to get in gear *now*. Not only was she interested in starting college again but she also wanted to start investing in her writing and speaking career.

I honestly wasn't opposed to Pam's growth, but I was adamantly opposed to the timing. Our preschool kids were younger than I wanted them to be when their mom would be gone part of the day. And I was busy—I did not want to have to take on the extra parenting responsibilities. I responded by being angry and belligerent.

For most of a year I criticized Pam for her decisions. I scheduled meetings with her so I could argue my case that she had her priorities out of balance. The bottom line was that I did not want to have to sacrifice for her. I wanted her to take a background role until all our children entered school. Then I would support her in the pursuit of her career.

I believed I could convince her to slow down her pursuits, so I reasoned with her at first. When she refused to back off from her goals, I became more adamant and less reasonable. I accused her of being selfish and not looking out for the needs of the family.

"You just don't understand," she would plead with me.

"Why? Because I'm not a woman, you think I don't understand what is happening with you?" I would shoot back.

"Yes. Because you're not a woman you will never understand the need to balance motherhood and career."

I hated hearing this from Pam, even though it was probably true. I didn't like being left out, and I especially didn't like being disregarded. What I failed to realize was that this whole thing was a courageous step of growth for Pam. She was feeling she would stagnate and never reach her potential. If she failed to discover what she could accomplish in life, she would feel cheated or disillusioned.

Another possible result would be that she might put too much pressure on the rest of us to make her happy. We would be responsible for filling the gaps left by her unfulfilled career desires.

We would *all* be at a disadvantage. Pam would be nagged by the haunting frustration of what could have been. I would be overwhelmed by the expectation to meet needs I was incapable of addressing. The kids would be overrun by the disappointment they would feel from Pam as she invested too much energy in their lives and tried to live vicariously through them. The only reasonable decision was for Pam to push ahead with this vital step of growth.

While Pam was going through this process, I was anything but supportive. I tried arguing, dragging my feet on assisting her, being unavailable when she needed help and talking with mentors about how to get Pam to change her mind. If Pam had not continually forgiven me, she would have lost focus and given in to my whining rather than following a strategic plan. Her strength put her way ahead of me in that phase of our life.

I finally caught up with her through a conversation I had with Jim Conway. "Jim," I asked impatiently, "how can I get Pam to slow down so our life will be easier? How can I get our life back under control?"

Jim looked at me across the table in the restaurant and asked this very probing question, "Bill, do you need to control your wife?"

I had to own up. I had wanted to be able to call the shots in Pam's life, and since I couldn't I had become stubborn. I was hoping that my moping and stubbornness would cause a positive change in our relationship. But negative input does not produce positive results.

To Pam's credit, she never gave up on what she needed to do. In retrospect, I see that she did the right thing. She needed to grow even if I didn't want to join her. Her incessant commitment to reaching her potential created enough stress in my life to keep me looking for an appropriate way to respond to her. It took a year—but I finally did it.

Since then Pam has become a more secure and productive person, and our home is running much more smoothly than it was when I was the sole provider. Her skills and talents are being used to help a lot of women, and her personal well-being makes the atmosphere in our home a more relaxed place to be. Because I responded by aggressively fathering our children, I have a close relationship with all three of my kids that is filled with memorable experiences. We have both become winners, but it would never have happened if Pam had not steadfastly competed for the privilege to grow.

Change Begets Change

Sarah longed for Johnny and herself to be connected spiritually and in tune with one another. She wanted them to get in the habit of reading the Bible and praying together as a couple. She had often asked

Johnny if they could get started, and she never got any active opposition. But he simply would not do it. He always made up reasons why other things had to be done, or he refused to get out of his favorite chair. For months she pushed, prodded and begged. When that didn't produce a plan for helping them exercise their spiritual life together, Sarah became frustrated with her marriage and started complaining about Johnny to her friends. Finally, she related her story to Pam and asked if there was anything that could be done to make Johnny respond.

"Pam, what do you think I should do to get Johnny to see our need to pray together?"

"First you've got to forgive Johnny for his laid-back style. If you don't, your emotions will paralyze you. Next, can you think of one thing that Johnny is doing that you could use to encourage him?"

Sarah thought for a few minutes and then said, "No, I can't think of anything Johnny is doing that causes me to think he will ever respond."

At this point Pam knew she had to take drastic measures. Sarah was spiraling downward in her respect for Johnny, and, as a result, her hope for a God-centered marriage was evaporating. Pam sent Sarah home with an assignment to actively forgive her husband and then find one thing she could appreciate. It took a few days, but Sarah finally came up with an answer.

"Well, Pam, I figured out one thing," she announced with a touch of sarcasm.

"Great, Sarah. What is it?"

"He's still there! That's it, he's still *there*," she repeated with obvious disappointment in her voice.

"Well, let's see if we can work with this. How can you use this characteristic to get Johnny's attention? How can you encourage him with the thought that he is there and hasn't left you?"

Pam explained to Sarah the "one hundred in one principle." If Sarah would take one hundred percent of her energy and put it into one positive characteristic, it would make Johnny feel appreciated for something he could do! Too often we use one hundred percent of our effort to point out the deficiencies in our spouses. Somehow we think that criticism will inspire others to respond with positive change, but most often it only leads to bitterness in us. Well, Sarah decided to give it a try.

Walking through the house, she noticed Johnny sitting in his favorite chair. By faith she said, "Hey Johnny, it does me good to see you sitting in that chair. It reminds me that I can always count on you to be there."

Johnny looked up at her with raised eyebrows and then just went back to watching television.

Sarah continued to find ways to encourage Johnny for his predictable, though boring, stability. "Johnny, I'm glad there are some things I can always count on. One of them is the fact that you will always be here."

Change didn't happen immediately, and Sarah had to be careful that she was not condescending in her encouragement, but eventually Johnny noticed. Sarah was in the living room one evening reading her Bible while Johnny was in the family room watching television. Johnny turned off the television and walked into the family room.

"What are you reading?" he asked.

"Are you sure you want to know?" Sarah responded hesitantly.

"Yes, I want to know."

"Well, I'm reading my Bible. I have some decisions ahead of me and I am finding insight by reading this."

"Really. Tell me about it." He sat down beside her.

Johnny listened intently as Sarah recounted the passages she was reading and how they related to the things that were going on in her life. Over the next few weeks Johnny started reading the Bible periodically and trying to do what he had seen Sarah do. He even sat down with Sarah a couple more times to discuss what the Bible had to say about their life together. Since that time, Johnny has been attending church regularly and slowly growing. He still has a lot to learn, and there is much that Sarah would like to see change, but their marriage is back in progress.

You Do Make a Difference

One of the strongest passages of Scripture on the subject of marriage relationships is found in Malachi 2:13-16:

> Another thing you do: You flood the LORD's altar with tears. You weep and wail because he no longer pays attention to your offerings or accepts them with pleasure from your hands. You ask, "Why?" It is because the LORD is acting as the witness between you and the wife of your youth, because you have broken faith with her, though she is your partner, the wife of your marriage covenant.
>
> Has not the LORD made them one? In flesh and spirit they are his. And why one? Because he was seeking godly offspring. So guard yourself in your spirit, and do not break faith with the wife of your youth.
>
> "I hate divorce," says the LORD God of Israel, "and I hate a man's covering himself with violence as well as with his garment," says the LORD Almighty.

So guard yourself in your spirit, and do not break faith.

The fascinating thing about this passage is that it is addressed to husbands, not couples! The implication is that the husband has the ability to make a difference in the marriage and usher God's approval into the family system. By implication, the wife has the same ability to bring about real change in a relationship if she is willing.

Where does the motivation come from to make the commitment to change even if your spouse is unwilling? The most obvious motivation in this passage is *the desire to "guard your spirit."* The men of the nation of Israel were distressed over the lack of vitality in their relationship with God. The prophet sums up their heartache: "You weep and wail because he no longer pays attention to your offerings or accepts them with pleasure from your hands" (v. 13). Their spiritual life was impotent as God appeared distant and unapproachable. Confusion had filled their hearts as their love of self overshadowed their once vibrant love for God. In their distress they cried out, "Why?" Part of God's response was to remind them, "Guard yourself in your spirit" (v. 15).

The second motivation is *the desire to use God's methods.* It is amazing that God has tied your relationship with him to your relationship with your spouse in an inseparable bond. He has made you one with your spouse. "She is your partner, the wife of your marriage covenant . . . the wife of your youth" (vv. 14-15). It is impossible for you to be the source of conflict with your spouse and be at peace with God. You may be in the distress of wondering where God is in your life. You may be feeling isolated or abandoned spiritually. This seems to be a very common experience for people. In many cases, the spiritual isolation you feel is an outgrowth of your unwillingness to mend the fences in your marriage relationship. If you would take a step toward your spouse, God would take a step toward you!

The third motivation listed here is *the health of the children you will bring into this world.* One of the main purposes of a godly life that results in an intimate marriage is the raising of godly offspring. "Has not the Lord made them one? In flesh and spirit they are his. And why one? Because he was seeking godly offspring" (v. 15).

As we mentioned earlier, kids pay the highest price for our lack of commitment and maturity. When you decide that you will courageously seek growth in your own life as well as in your marriage, your kids reap the greatest benefits. Your convictions and strength of character are multiplied in their hearts, and they get propelled forward in their love for God and their ability to have healthy relationships. If you selfishly put your own needs ahead of theirs, they are propelled backward in their development; wounds are created in their hearts that must be healed before they can discover healthy relationships. Archibald Hart points out, "The anger and resentment between parents, which is so prevalent in most divorces, creates intense fear in the child. The younger the child, the more damage this climate of hostility can do."[2]

Broken marriage relationships create distance in a spiritual relationship with God and leave kids in a broken state. This is part of why God says, "I hate divorce." As you agree with God, you are motivated to adopt the same mindset Jesus brought with him to earth. In your heart you will discover the desire to "do nothing out of selfish ambition or vain conceit, but in humility consider others better than yourselves. Each of you should look not only to your own interests, but also to the interests of others. Your attitude should be the same as that of Christ Jesus" (Phil 2:3-5).

But this attitude was not just taught; it was lived out. When it comes to our salvation, Jesus was the only one working on it when he went to the cross. "God demonstrates his own love for us in this: While we were still sinners, Christ died for us" (Rom 5:8).

We were wandering and lost in our own selfish desires. We were not seeking after God or his way of life. We were distracted in our temptations and pathetically attempting to control life. In the midst of our foolishness, God showed his love with actions. "For God so loved the world that he gave his one and only Son, that whoever believes in him shall not perish but have eternal life" (Jn 3:16).

The example of Jesus is the one thing that is big enough to inspire selfless sacrifice on our part. He gave his life on the cross to pay for our sins long before we reconciled with him. He pursues us in love and shares his riches with all who respond. Therefore, when we sacrifice for his sake, we do so with the hope that he takes note and will reward us eventually. Any other motivation leads us to feel we are just caving in to our weaknesses or to the abuse of others. You will run the race of self-sacrifice only if you run behind Jesus.

> Therefore, since we are surrounded by such a great cloud of witnesses, let us throw off everything that hinders and the sin that so easily entangles, and let us run with perseverance the race marked out for us. Let us fix our eyes on Jesus, the author and perfecter of our faith, who for the joy set before him endured the cross, scorning its shame, and sat down at the right hand of the throne of God. Consider him who endured such opposition from sinful men, so that you will not grow weary and lose heart. (Heb 12:1-3)

Everything you do makes a difference!

Focus on the Heart
Lord, help me to believe that I can make a difference in my relationship with my spouse. Show me that I am just as powerful to make changes as my spouse is,

because you are with me. Give me the confidence to say, "I can do everything through him who gives me strength" (Phil 4:13).

A Step Toward Love

Choose one area of your life that you have been wanting to change; decide to get started now! Commit the plan to prayer. Commit the plan to paper. Commit the plan to action. Then ask God to use the change in you to produce change in your marriage.

Eleven

Keeping the
Slate Clean

T*wo people who try to set up a life together are guaranteed to have conflict.*
You will make numerous mistakes with one another and will hurt each
other on a regular basis. These mistakes will range from forgetting to
buy milk on the way home to forgetting your anniversary. They will
vary from having a poor memory to having an affair. You will put your
foot in your mouth, and you may put your family in bankruptcy.
Whether the mistakes—your own and your partner's—are big or
small, you must manage your reactions so the mistakes do not define
the quality or direction of your relationship.

Forgive Everything!
The best marriage partners have mastered the art of forgiveness. They
have faced the reality that everyone is imperfect. They have settled it
ahead of time: They will expect mistakes and will forgive each and
every one of them.

Every decision to not forgive becomes a thorn bush that is planted
between the two of you. Plant one, and you can still see over it. Plant a

whole garden of thorn bushes, and you will get hurt each time you try to approach each other. Of course, a big violation can plant a huge thorn bush, but a series of small hurts can create just as thorny a garden. If small infractions are left unattended, they will grow until they become a collective entanglement of hurt feelings and mistrust. The thorn bushes you allow to take root between the two of you discourage healthy interaction and prevent corrective conversations.

You may be reading this and saying, "There are just some things I cannot forgive." If you are tempted to think this way, consider Keith and Linda's journey.

Keith and Linda received a harsh wake-up call in their relationship. They were both hoping the painful memories could be buried. Keith had an affair early in their marriage. Now he wanted desperately to just move forward by quieting Linda's fears with the promise that his affair was over. "It's over. Really. I'll never see her again." But rather than deal with the affair, Keith tried to deny its effects.

Linda had married late in life and had always wanted a family of her own, so Keith thought he could divert attention from the affair by encouraging Linda to have a baby. They'd only been married for six months when the affair had begun, and now Keith thought they could just chalk up the affair to a bad start.

"Please, honey. I love you," Keith added with repentance in his voice. "I'll never wander again. I promise. Please, really. I am sorry."

Linda ran it over and over in her mind for the next several days. Keith seemed contrite enough. There were the flowers, the cards, the apologies.

One day she said, hesitating, "OK, you can come back."

Linda was elated when her pregnancy test came back positive. She felt free, like they had a new start, another chance at love. She felt on top of the world—until the day the phone rang. Keith's old girlfriend was on the line.

"I don't know if you know," the girlfriend said smugly, "but in a few months I'm going to have Keith's baby." Their straw house of denial exploded.

For the rest of her pregnancy, Linda agonized over the devastation in her heart while Keith incessantly apologized, begging her to stay in the marriage. She wasn't sure what she was going to do. *I think I'll wait until after the baby is born to decide,* she thought to herself. *No, I think I'll wait until Keith's girlfriend delivers before I decide.*

Keith kept begging for forgiveness, but Linda wasn't sure if she could forgive this time. The strain on the relationship heightened, and not even the delivery of a healthy baby girl gave her hope for the relationship. Linda lived in a state of indecision for months. She was neither happy nor ready to leave.

"I just need some time," Linda said in resignation as she finally took the baby and moved out.

As time passed, Linda became agonizingly aware of her desire to have her family intact. She knew this might be more than she and Keith could handle, but she still wanted him to come back and pursue a healthy relationship with her. Keith was consistently asking her permission to come back, but Linda was holding out, because she didn't want to go back to what they used to have.

Choose Well the Hills You Die On

Forgiveness needs discernment to finish its course. Some issues are so critical to the health of your relationship that they need direct and immediate attention. Other issues do not warrant much attention at all. One of the keys to success in love relationships is to prioritize your discussions. If you make an issue out of everything, your spouse will give up because it will feel as if life is being scrutinized under a microscope. If you make a big deal out of the little issues, it will appear that you do not have the discernment to be trusted. If you trivialize the big issues, you will seem insensitive and incapable of a mature relationship. The key is to choose wisely the issues you will forgive and not bring up for discussion, and the issues you will forgive but also will seek to discuss so that change can be negotiated.

Here are some questions to ask yourself that will help you decide if the offense needs to be brought up for discussion:

☐ Is the change I would like to see in my spouse realistic?

☐ Will discussion of this issue make a significant difference in the way my spouse and I interact?

☐ Is there any benefit to be derived from discussing this issue?

☐ Am I discussing this issue because I honestly want to improve our relationship and not just because I want my spouse to feel bad?

☐ If my spouse were to agree with me on this issue, would we feel closer to each other?

If you arrive at positive answers to these questions, then the issue on your mind is probably worth talking about. If you get negative answers in your heart, you probably want to talk about this issue out of insecurity rather than a healthy desire to see your relationship grow. The issues that will only grind on your spouse need to be erased with forgiveness rather than fostered by conversations in which no one will win. The issues that will fester in your heart need to be talked through so that a resolution can be reached.

Linda had run this over and over in her mind. She wanted Keith to work together with her on this. She knew she wouldn't be able to trust Keith if he came home without directly confronting the problems in their relationship. She needed something tangible to anchor her trust to—so in an act of desperation Linda surprised Keith with the statement, "If you want to give this relationship a real try, come to the marriage conference our church is hosting in a few weeks."

"OK. I'm not sure what two strangers talking about all these perfect marriages can do for us, but if that's what you want, I'll come."

Keith and Linda did come to our marriage conference. A year later, they came to another one. Linda ran up to me (Pam) before it even began and said,

> You just have to know! Last year we were separated when we came. I didn't have much hope, and Keith had even less. But I just had to tell you—the stuff you shared on forgiveness—it really works. My husband had had an affair. His girlfriend and I were pregnant at the same time. I didn't think I could ever forgive him, much less ever love him again, but I do. And he loves me.

Last year after the conference, we found out that his girlfriend was neglecting and abusing his son, so we decided to go to court to get custody. I can't believe it, but I love him. I forgive Keith and I want to raise that little boy as if he were my own. I can't believe the change in Keith either. He never used to talk to or care about me, but now he does. He said he had a hard time living with me because he was reminded every day of the hurt he'd caused with the affair. But what you shared helped him forgive himself too! I can't thank you enough. God used your words to bring his forgiveness and healing to our lives.

Give In to Humility

One of the ways to clean the slate in your relationship and keep it clean is to make humble choices. We all want to hide our flaws and deny our shortcomings. Admitting we need help feels like a statement of weakness, so we cover it up with anger or pride. Each of us is faced with the choice to either alienate ourselves from our spouse with pride or foster intimacy by humbly admitting that we are not self-sufficient.

Larry had an especially difficult time giving up his pride and humbly admitting his needs. He wanted desperately to go to his grandmother's funeral and take part in the Catholic communion service, but he hadn't stepped foot in a church in years. When he went to confession and the priest heard that it had been ten years since his last confession, he dropped his Bible on the floor. In shock and disbelief he said, "I don't want to hear your confession. Ten years, that will take forever! Do you have a wife? Kids?"

Larry nodded yes.

"Do you take them to church?" the priest inquired.

Larry shook his head no.

"Then instead of the usual confession and penitence, can you just make a vow to take your wife and kids to church?"

Larry was feeling very uncomfortable at this point and was willing to vow anything just to get out of there. But he didn't take himself, or anyone else, to church for a long time.

Months later, a man trying to start a new church in the neighborhood came by Larry's house and introduced himself. Larry couldn't believe his own ears when he heard himself invite the man into his home. Over coffee, Larry began asking the man questions about God.

"Come to church Sunday," the young pastor added as he said farewell to Larry.

The next weekend, Larry attended that church with his wife and family. At the end of the service, the man said a prayer that invited people to come forward if they wanted a personal relationship with God. Larry felt he should go, but he didn't, and neither did his wife or any of his family. Afterward, Larry spoke with the pastor and told him, "I feel like I should have responded to the invitation at the end, but I was kind of scared."

"Think about it this week," the pastor challenged. "If you have questions, call me. And I'll see you next Sunday. All right?"

Larry nodded yes.

That was the week all hell broke loose. The next Saturday evening, Larry began drinking. As he became increasingly irritated with his wife, Beverly, he called his mother-in-law, ranting and raving. He then picked a fight with Beverly that escalated into an angry attack. He chased her through the house and threw a TV set at her. The set smashed into pieces as it missed her by inches.

She ran to the phone to call her mom.

"Beverly, leave him!" her mom shouted into the phone. "He's acting like the devil himself! Please get out of there!" But Beverly didn't have to. Larry was speeding out of the driveway and heading to a friend's house. He and his drinking buddy sat up all night talking.

In the morning Larry looked up, saw the clock on the wall and stood up to leave for church. He felt like he needed to get to church or he'd die.

"Don't go," his friend called out, but it was too late. Larry was gone.

Larry marched down the aisle of the church and sat in the same row as Beverly. It felt to him like everyone in the church was staring at him, and he was sure they all knew what a jerk he'd been. During the entire service he sat praying that the pastor would give the same invitation.

When he did, Larry stood to his feet and stretched an open hand to his wife. She put her hand in his and they walked to the front to pray, looking for a fresh start.

It was like a new beginning. Soon after, as they were lying in bed together, Larry said, "There are some things you need to know. I need to tell them to you and ask for your forgiveness."

Then Larry worked his way through a long list. Beverly was so impressed at his honesty and vulnerability that she joined in and listed the things she had done to violate their relationship. There in the dark quiet of their room, they lay in each other's arms and humbly extended forgiveness to one another.

"I don't want anything to come between us!" Larry said as the tears rolled down his cheeks.

Larry and Beverly discovered a whole new life that day. The commitment to love one another was joined with tears, relief, joy, intimacy, sexual oneness and freedom to admit wrong through the courageous act of forgiveness. That was years ago. Now Beverly and Larry share their story with whoever will listen. We met them when we were both guests on the television program *His Place.*

"It's so great now," Beverly says with a gleam in her eyes. "God made our love possible. My husband went from wanting to murder me to wanting to cherish me—overnight. That is an amazing thing. Forgiveness is amazing."

"Give up your rights," adds Larry enthusiastically. "For most couples it isn't the huge or dramatic things that need forgiven. It is the daily un-dealt-with disappointments and disillusionments. It's the unmet expectations and unresolved feelings of anger, frustration and inadequacy. For most couples, marriage and love die slowly. Like an untreated cancer, neglect eats away at intimacy until one day all feelings of love, and all hope for rekindling them, are gone. Little unresolved issues turn into huge wedges in our relationships, and we are driven apart. It is only in giving up our right to be angry, hurt or disappointed that we can get the relationship back."

Sorting Out Ordinary Struggles

Most couples do not experience struggles as drastic as Keith and Linda's or Larry and Beverly's, but the stress of life provides plenty of opportunities to offend each other. When these offenses occur, they can easily be made worse by attempting to assign motives to the behavior you have witnessed.

I (Bill) was recently working around the house trying to get caught up. I had made a mental list of the order in which I was going to tackle the tasks. Pam was away from the house doing errands, and I thought I had things in order.

When she came home, the first thing Pam did was to walk up to me and ask if I had made a certain phone call I had promised to make.

I immediately got offended. I was tired from a busy week and was already struggling to keep my attitude positive. When Pam came in proclaiming her expectations, I immediately started guessing at her motives. *She doesn't care at all about me. She knew I would be upset if she barged in with her agenda today. I thought she was on my side, but it's obvious that she just wants to take from me, like everybody else.*

For a brief few moments I actually thought that was true. But then I realized that kind of thinking was crazy. I would have to read Pam's mind to know any of this. I had to talk to myself to adjust my attitude. *Bill, rethink this. Pam has been your most active cheerleader. She has always believed in you. And, by the way, what would she accomplish by making your day miserable? She is probably just tired like you and didn't realize what your needs were today.*

Because I was willing to admit that I did not know Pam's motives, I was able to think through what I should say to Pam. I was able to stop and focus on her behavior. Her behavior did not look nearly as sinister as her supposed motives had. If I had remained focused on what I thought her actions meant, I would have had a miserable day, and a wedge would have been put between Pam and me because of the question, "Bill, did you make that phone call?" After pulling my thoughts together I approached Pam.

"Pam," I asked tentatively, "Do you know why I got offended earlier when you asked me about the phone call?"

"No," she said with a surprised look on her face.

"I was already having trouble juggling my day. Your question caused me to shuffle my whole list, and I lost focus."

"I was wondering. I was just trying to help. I think we are both just really tired. I didn't sense your need, and you couldn't handle my question."

I was dumbfounded. She understood completely. She sensed that I was fatigued and could easily be overwhelmed. At the same time, she wasn't doing much better than I was, and so she couldn't process my needs. That realization drained the venom out of her actions. I was no longer irritated, and I certainly didn't feel like accusing her of taking advantage of me.

If I had accused Pam of her supposed bad motives, we would have had a very ugly day. She would have felt attacked and misunderstood and probably would have defended herself. She might even have had a few choice words to say about how far off base I was. I would have responded with more accusations or with an even more defensive posture. The resulting argument would have been a huge irritation to both of us (and to anyone within hearing distance). When we were done, we would have been left wondering why we had the fight in the first place.

When you venture into the realm of trying to identify your spouse's motives, you move into arenas that are beyond your ability. It is far better to comment on your spouse's *behavior* and let the *motives* be revealed by your spouse.

Some guidelines for commenting on the behavioral inconsistencies of your spouse are:

1. Make eye contact. If you seem uninterested in your spouse as a person, it is unlikely you will make any headway in talking. Look him or her steadily in the eyes, but not with a blank stare. Deliberately say with your facial expressions that you are concerned about the well-being of your relationship.

2. Focus your words on how the behavior affects you. Instead of saying, "You were so rude to make that appointment without consulting me," say, "When you make appointments without checking with me, I feel devalued and disregarded." The joy of marriage is that everything your spouse does has a profound effect on you, but your spouse may not always be sensitive to this influence.

3. Choose your tone of voice. A harsh tone of voice is likely to bring a defensive reaction. A sensitive or inquisitive tone will likely open a door for a new level of conversation that will cause your relationship to grow beyond the individual issue you are bringing up.

4. Find an introduction. Corrective conversations usually fall apart at the beginning of the discussion. Couples don't decide ahead of time how they will begin these potentially contentious interactions. If you begin the conversation in a way that your spouse thinks is inappropriate, you will get off track and spend the time arguing over procedure rather than the issue at hand. The key to finding good introductions is to develop signals that prepare one another for the upcoming conversation. If you discover signals that work, you will find it easier to have honest conversations. If, on the other hand, you surprise each other every time you have a difficult subject to bring up, there is no way the conversation is going to be successful.

Pam and I address this issue in our relationship by using the phrase, "Something I love about you is driving me crazy." This sets a positive tone for the conversation. It says, "I love you, and I know I will once again discover why, if we only take time to talk." It gives us permission to deal with bad stuff in the midst of a good relationship. It gives us the freedom to not have to be perky and on top of life all the time.

Shortcomings and bad days need not threaten the sense of well-being in our love. At times, these otherwise difficult discussions can seem like treasure hunts. We know something good is buried behind a bad attitude or an outrageous reaction. Even though these conversations are not easy, they often turn out to be worth the effort of digging under the surface of frustration to find the treasure hidden in our hearts.

5. Agree on passwords. You need some escape hatches for conversations that go haywire. These discussions are a challenge, and nobody does them right all the time. When a well-intentioned conversation takes a nosedive into an emotional abyss, you need a way to start over. If it is plummeting in a free fall of nonsense, you have to call a halt and just begin again. A password is a phrase the two of you have agreed on ahead of time that alerts you to the reality that this conversation is racing toward a dead end.

Your password may be as simple as the phrase, "This is not working. Can we start over?" Or it may be more customized to your relationship.

Some friends of ours have an interesting dynamic in their relationship. He is a driven businessman who is great at getting things done. He lives by a list and moves obstacles out of his way rather than going around them. She, on the other hand, is a sensitive artist who has deep insight into the nuances of life. She likes to experience life rather than conquer it. When they try to talk, she often feels run over by him. They have chosen to use the phrase "Beep, Beep!" from the Roadrunner cartoon. When she says this phrase she is saying, "You are running me over, and I'm about to bail out of this conversation." When he says this phrase, he is saying, "I must be running you over because I can tell you are shutting down on me."

One password that has been especially effective for Pam and me is "It's not you. It's not me. It's just life." It started when we were having an especially strenuous time in life and both had the feeling that we should be handling it better. As a result, we were having consistent arguments about who needed to change. No matter how much we tried, we couldn't change enough to make the stress go away. The fact is we had three children, growing financial needs, career pressures, and a significant network of friends and family we wanted to keep in touch with. One day we were talking over our life, feeling guilty about our inability to master all our responsibilities, when it occurred to me (Bill)—*this is just the way life is!* I looked at Pam and said, "It's not you. It's not me. It's just life."

She looked back at me with determination on her face and said, "It has to be one of us. We can't just accept this."

I was adamant at this point. "Pam, look at our life. Which of our responsibilities are you going to get rid of? We can't give back one of the kids. We can't quit our careers, or our kids won't eat. We don't want to lose contact with our friends and family. So it is just life!"

Again she insisted, "There must be a way to point the finger at one of us. One of us must need to change. There has to be a way to assign responsibility for this." Then she just stopped in her tracks as the realization overcame her. She got a sly little grin on her face as she repeated, "It's not you. It's not me. It's just life!"

Successful passwords have a few common characteristics. First, there is agreement that this password will work. If you decide to use a password but your spouse does not agree, it will only make the argument more intense. Second, it needs to express mutual respect. (If you choose to say, "This is who I am. Deal with it!" you can be assured that the cold shoulder will be delivered directly to your doorstep.) Third, try to relate the password to a good memory or a positive thought in your relationship. It could be from a favorite movie, joke or story. Or it could be a reminder of something that happened on your honeymoon or a favorite vacation. Finally, humor helps. When tensions are high, the serious issues can be easier if the two of you share a good laugh.

Stay Out of the Shadows

During one of our disagreements, Bill said to me, "Pam, how long am I going to have to prove my love to you? Your dad wasn't there for you, but I will be. I will always be there! I love you, Pam. How long is the shadow of your dad going to hang over our relationship?"

Up until that point, I had not realized that I didn't fully trust my husband, even though he had been consistently trustworthy. His words exposed an invisible wedge that had the potential to drive us apart. That invisible wedge is a pain I have carried in my heart for a long time. It has to do with my dad. He was a wonderful man—when he wasn't drinking. But when he was under the influence of alcohol, he was unpredictable and unreliable. He was actively involved with my life and was the hit of the neighborhood when I was young. As I grew, however, he became more dependent upon alcohol and his actions were more and more erratic and embarrassing. I got to the point where I didn't know which dad to expect, so I quit depending on him altogether.

A good example of my dad's embarrassing behavior happened during our engagement. We had met with Dad briefly to discuss the wedding, and we set a date to visit him at his house. On the way up I related to Bill that my father had a habit of doing or being hurtful, violent or embarrassing to us kids when he was drinking.

When we arrived at Dad's place he wasn't home. He was out water skiing and drinking with his buddies. When Dad skied, Dad drank. When Dad drank and skied he would get in a barbecue kind of mood. But when you drink and barbecue, what you end up with is a burnt offering. Dad plunked the unknown meat in front of Bill and me, and we all figured out quickly that it was inedible. So I said to Dad, "That's OK. We came to see you. We don't care what we eat. How about I just order a pizza?"

Well, the pizza arrived and we sat down to eat. I still hoped that the night might be redeemed into some form of quality time. Instead, because Dad had drunk so much, he suddenly became violently sick, and the contents of his stomach came out all over the pizza. I was mortified. I remember trying to fling myself in front of my new fiancé to somehow protect him from the scene.

Bill has never done anything as outrageous as this! But I still have struggled with trusting him. It is as if I'm waiting for him to blow up just like my dad did. I had a good childhood with my dad, and then our relationship deteriorated. I don't mean to have that same sense of timing with Bill, but it takes work to keep telling myself, *Bill is not like Dad. He has a great track record, so judge him on his own merits, not your dad's.*

Whenever we think about this event, we tell ourselves, *This is our life; we can write the script the way we want. We cannot ignore the past or our current struggles, but we do not have to be slaves to them.* The other couples in this book have also discovered that they can rewrite the script of their relationship if they preface it with forgiveness.

How about you? How do you want the story of your marriage to be written?

Focus on the Heart

Oh Lord, help me to avoid measuring the present by the past. Give me wisdom to keep the small issues small and the big issues big. Teach me how to fight for our relationship rather than against my spouse.

A Step Toward Love

Make a list of three or four possible signals or passwords that you and your spouse could use to start sensitive, encouraging conversations. Make an appointment with your spouse to discuss your ideas, and see if you can agree on a couple of signals that will enhance your marriage.

Twelve

The Power of
Forgiveness

I*n an interview, Danna gave the details behind the moment when she learned* a life-shattering fact.

A heaviness in my heart and spirit enveloped me as I strolled toward the mailbox.

After years of banging away in the corporate rat race, I had finally taken an impulsive plunge into my own business. From my husband's perspective, it appeared more like a suicidal jump into an empty swimming pool. Actually, Lewis was angry—and hurt that I would take action without his blessing. It was something I'd been talking about for months, even years. I thought I'd told him how important this was to me. He thought he'd expressed the need to have a well-defined plan before leaving the perks and security of a management position.

He thought, she thought . . . Rationalization was a mastered skill I had acquired during my "superwoman" years. *I* thought the time was right. *I* needed this change, and now was the time. *I* had negotiated a severance package. Why couldn't *he* emotionally support me in this?

Was this why we were experiencing new struggles in our married life?

For almost ten years I had felt loved and supported. I knew Lew was my best friend. We had always felt connected. We laughed. We called ourselves soulmates. But recently I felt as if I was watching our relationship slowly disintegrate before my eyes.

Shortly after I announced my resignation, Lew left on an extended business trip. He had always traveled a lot. But this time he would be gone twelve days. The days before his departure were a whirlwind of activities as I developed the marketing materials for my new endeavor—videotaping and editing, brochures and business plans filled my waking moments. I apologized profusely for overbooking my schedule and not being available to drive him to the airport. A quick hug and kiss . . . and he was gone. Again I rationalized, *These twelve days will be a great time to get all my work organized; then we can have some quality time.*

That had been less than a month earlier. Lew had called me from his business trip sounding oddly detached. He expressed an emptiness and concerns for where our relationship was going. I responded with a mixture of surprise and anxiety. What was he saying?

A week that should have passed quickly in all my busyness became a string of endless days and sleepless nights. I became obsessed with the possibilities. Was it another woman? Just plain discontentment? Or was he simply falling out of love?

The mailman had just driven away. I noticed a bundle of letters sitting on top of our community mailbox. *Hmm . . . odd that he would drive off without them,* I thought. These must be the letters that had been in the drop for outgoing mail. I picked up the stack, which was bundled with a rubber band and too thick to stuff into the narrow outgoing mail slot. *I'd better get these back in there.*

I removed the rubber band and inserted the first letter, the second, the third. My heart skipped a beat. The next letter looked like a greeting card in its soft lavender envelope. The precise printing was easy to discern. It was Lew's. It was addressed to a woman.

My heart began to pound. I started to slip it into the outgoing mail slot. I really tried. I just could not let go. Hurriedly I crammed in the other letters. The lavender menace stayed stuck to my left hand.

Inside my front door, I collapsed on the staircase. What was I thinking? What did I think I was going to do with this letter? I stared for several minutes at the printing I knew so well. Something was wrong . . . very, very wrong.

I spoke to myself in a series of fragmented thoughts: *I have to know . . . I can't just go out and mail it. I must be crazy. It's probably a thank-you note to one of his business contacts. She's probably a grandmother! If I open it and it's nothing, I'll have to tell him what a crazy fool I am. If I open it and it's something* . . . That thought stuck in my throat like a tennis ball.

"Let me be a crazy fool, Lord . . . just let me be the fool." I ripped open the letter. It was one of those wispy, sophisticated cards with a subtle message like "I Thought of You Today and. . . ." My heart crumbled to a million pieces in one split second, and I hadn't read a single word. The note that followed explained a lot of things. I had been blinded by Lew's excuses and smoke screens.

During that time of pain, I prayed that God would do surgery on my heart. I became convicted of my own complacency and personal ambitions. As Lew withdrew more, I began to hunger for the best friend and soulmate I once knew. In his perfect timing, God profoundly delivered truth to me that spring day. His divine intervention exposed the truth that Lew so desperately needed to confess.[1]

Believe in God's Ability to Heal Your Heart

A healthy marriage will certainly strengthen any individual. But life is fragile, and everybody falls short. For a while we may think that we have it made and that life is manageable, but it will never be contained or controlled. As a result, there will be times when life suddenly becomes overwhelming. The news of an affair tears away at your heart. Cruel words from your spouse stab you like a sharp knife. Staggering responsibilities at work cause you to lose focus in your marriage and neglect the one you said was the most important person in your life. Add to this the general unhappiness you feel during times of change and the nagging inconsistencies that haunt your thinking and desires, and the only reasonable conclusion is that *each of us needs more help in our lives than a spouse can provide.*

A husband can find great pleasure in his wife, but she cannot calm the fears that resonate in his soul. She is the right companion for life, but no wife can tame a man's struggle with the aggressive temptations that chase men. Many happily married men still struggle with pornography. A lot of husbands wrestle with simmering anger and desperately hope it does not fly out of control and hurt their loved ones. A man who hates to be alone and is insecure without encouraging feedback from a loving woman is not unusual—he is typical. We men pretend to be self-sufficient and fully capable, but deep within we are aware of our need for God.

A wife finds great security in the strong and considerate attention a husband gives to her. He provides safety and companionship that no other woman could bring to her heart. When a husband genuinely cares for his wife, she senses an almost intoxicating warmth in her soul. But even the most secure wife may struggle with depression or anxiety. It is common for a wife to feel a need to control the lives of her family even when the family is cooperative and kind. It is also common for a woman's heart to drift when her husband gets busy. If she is not careful, she may become emotionally captivated by another man who has time to listen. We women pretend to be stable and to possess convictions as strong as iron, but the fact is we need the power of God within us to keep our hearts from wandering.

Danna and Lew were both hurting. They had drifted apart emotionally, and deep needs were floating in their hearts demanding to be met. Having acted on those unstable needs, they needed to be healed as individuals before their relationship could be repaired.

Danna continued:

I gave God all the broken pieces that day. I wasn't sure how he would put them back together. Before I went into my husband's office and dialed his pager number, I fell into a heap and prayed, *Lord, only You know the truth. Only you know how to put us back together again. You know the role I have played, you know how far Lew has crossed the line. What I know is that I love you and I love my husband. I also know I am capable of the same sin; I crossed that line in my first marriage and almost again with Lew.*

In my first marriage, I had chosen to walk away, to cross the line and seek recognition and identity in men other than my husband. That had resulted in a divorce of my own making in 1984—a divorce that deeply wounded my children and their father. I never understood their pain or my sin until I was on the other side of the situation.

Ten years later, when I met Lewis, he was all I could ever imagine in a lover, a soulmate and husband. And now our marriage was in terrible danger.

With his fullness of grace, God delivered to me a spirit of complete forgiveness. In that moment of betrayal and pain, his love poured out on me mercy and compassion. I remembered the verse, "A broken and contrite heart . . . [the LORD] will not despise" (Ps 51:17).

The phone ringing jolted me into the present. Lewis was returning my page. The 9-1-1 code had caught his immediate attention. "Lewis, I read a letter today . . . I shouldn't have opened your personal mail. I just had to. I love you. I forgive you. Please come home."[2]

Believe in God's Plan for Eternity

Danna and Lew were willing to pursue reconciliation with each other because they had already been through a process of reconciliation with even farther-reaching implications. They had come to grips with their need for an eternal Savior. Years before, they had accepted that they had offended God with their selfish living and they needed to be forgiven. They were willing to confess their self-centered approach to life, repent of their reliance upon their own resources and accept God's plan as the right way to live. They committed to believing the following statements and bringing their daily decisions and actions in line with them.

God's Statement of Love to Us
"I LOVE YOU, AND I HAVE A PLAN FOR YOU."

☐ *I came to give life—life in all its fullness. (Jn 10:10)*

☐ *I came so they can have real and eternal life, more and better life than they ever dreamed of. (Jn 10:10 The Message)*

☐ *For God loved the world so much that he gave his only Son. God gave his Son so that whoever believes in him may not be lost, but have eternal life. (Jn 3:16)*

"I KNOW YOU ARE IMPERFECT, SO YOU ARE SEPARATED FROM MY LOVE; OUR RELATIONSHIP IS BROKEN. YOU ARE IN NEED OF FORGIVENESS."

☐ *All people have sinned and are not good enough for God's glory. (Rom 3:23)*

☐ *We've compiled this long and sorry record as sinners . . . and proved that we are utterly incapable of living the glorious lives God wills for us. (Rom 3:23 The Message)*

☐ *And when a person knows the right thing to do, but does not do it, then he is sinning. (Jas 4:17)*

☐ *It is your evil that has separated you from your God. Your sins cause him to turn away from you. (Is 59:2)*

"I LOVE YOU, SO I, WHO AM PERFECT, PAID THE PRICE FOR YOUR IMPERFECTION SO I COULD FORGIVE YOU AND RESTORE OUR RELATIONSHIP."

☐ *But Christ died for us while we were still sinners. In this way God shows his great love for us. We have been made right with God by the blood of Christ's death. So through Christ we will surely be saved from God's anger. I mean that while we were God's enemies, God made friends with us through the death of his Son. Surely, now that we are God's friends, God will save us through his Son's life. (Rom 5:8-10)*

☐ *Christ had no sin. But God made him become sin. God did this for us so that in Christ we could become right with God. (2 Cor 5:21)*

☐ *Christ himself died for you. And that one death paid for your sins. He was not guilty, but he died for those who are guilty. He did this to bring you all to God. (1 Pet 3:18)*

☐ *The greatest love a person can show is to die for his friends. (Jn 15:13)*

"TO INITIATE THIS NEW RELATIONSHIP, ALL YOU NEED TO DO IS TO ACCEPT MY PAYMENT FOR YOUR IMPERFECTION. I CANNOT MAKE YOU LOVE ME; THAT IS YOUR CHOICE."

☐ *I mean that you have been saved by grace because you believe you did not save yourselves. It was a gift from God. You cannot brag that you are saved by the work you have done. God has made us what we are. In Christ Jesus, God made us new people. (Eph 2:8-10)*

☐ *If you use your mouth to say, "Jesus is LORD" and if you believe in your heart God raised Jesus from death, then you will be saved. (Rom 10:9)*

☐ *And this is eternal life: that men can know you, the only true God, and that men can know Jesus Christ, the One you sent. (Jn 17:3)*

Danna and Lew talked to God. They told him that they had been wrong to exclude him from their lives and that they now wanted to be forgiven. You too can accept God's love for you. But you need to talk to him and tell him you need him. Tell him you've been wrong and you need his forgiveness to give you hope for eternity and for life here on earth. If you have never made this commitment to Christ, here is a sample prayer:

> Jesus, I am sorry I have chosen to live apart from you. I want you in my life. I know that I need to be forgiven for excluding you from my life and for thinking I could do it all on my own. I accept the payment of love you gave for me by your death on the cross. Please come into my life and teach me how to live. Thank you for being my best friend and my God.

Your willingness to let Christ be the center of your life is the greatest step you will ever take toward being a great marriage partner. The biggest needs of your life can be addressed by Jesus, so that the needs you expect your spouse to meet are realistic. Not only will you have eternal hope because of his forgiveness but you will have inner strength to forgive your spouse on a regular basis.

Danna explains how her relationship with Christ made it possible for her to seek healing rather than revenge. She also describes how her marriage got into trouble because both she and Lew were allowing other priorities to supersede the work of Christ in their lives.

> In part, the journey to restore our marriage had actually started for me years ago when I decided that divorce was no longer in my vocabulary. That, coupled with my commitment back in 1991 to follow God's principles, did not allow me to explore any option other than forgiveness and restoration.

The day I found out about Lew's affair was a testing time for me.
Was I going to scream and yell and demand my rights or vengeance?
Or was I going to seek the face of Jesus, follow his lead and give what
he had given me—forgiveness? My heart felt as if it would crumble
inside my chest, my mind raced with all the imaginations of what Lew
had done—but my spirit said, "Forgive."

Forgiveness isn't an exercise in self-righteousness. It is an act of
obedience. I am no saint. I was angry, I was bitter, I was hurting. But I
chose forgiveness. How could I do anything less when Jesus has forgiven me of every single sin I have *ever* committed?

At first when I cried or mistrusted Lew, he would angrily shout at
me, "I thought you forgave me!" We both learned that forgiving and
forgetting are two very different things. Trust and respect had been
broken. They would take time to heal.[3]

Believe in God's Ability to Heal Your Relationship

The merging of two lives is a challenge for every couple. For those who
have experienced difficult interruptions to the process of intimacy, the
challenge is even greater. There is no eraser for the events of the past,
and there is no vaccine for the flaws in each of your hearts. As a result,
some parts of your relationship need to be undergirded by God's
strength, and some parts just plain need healing. In Acts 28:27 God
calls each of us to a place where he can heal:

> For this people's heart has become calloused;
>   they hardly hear with their ears,
>   and they have closed their eyes.
> Otherwise they might see with their eyes,
>   hear with their ears,
>   understand with their hearts
> and turn, and I would heal them.

Danna recounts the healing that God performed in her relationship
with Lew.

Initially, Lew tried to hide from his sin. He wanted to change churches,
neglect friendships and avoid talking about what had happened. I

learned an important lesson in those early months. I could not control anything about our situation except my own thoughts and actions! I had to do what God called *me* to do and trust *him* to convict Lew.

The next year I experienced my most profound spiritual growth as I prayed and turned Lew and our relationship over to God. Prayer was the glue that held our relationship together as God was mending the broken pieces of our hearts.

But God *is* faithful, and he *does* answer prayer. A very grounded man came alongside Lew to become his accountability partner (and I didn't even have to nag him—it happened without any effort on my part). Lew also participated in Promise Keepers for the first time. He came home a changed man, a broken man, a godly man.

Lew immediately began to face the issues. He acknowledged the temptations that face a traveling businessman—something that he had always denied. He faced his sexual lust and fine lines of rationalization. He took the initiative to ask for forgiveness from friends and pastors he had deceived. We stepped down from leadership in our church and asked for prayer as we sought restoration.

Christian counseling was an important part of our journey back to wholeness. As we first entered our counselor's office, I was so ready for her to help Lew change. Much to my surprise she focused on *me* first! We are each accountable for our own choices and sin. Yet this very wise woman helped me see my role in making our marriage a true and lasting relationship.

The most important thing Lew let me do was ask questions and grieve. Once he fully understood I had forgiven him and was committed to our marriage, he felt secure enough to allow me to hurt. The pain of his infidelity began to diminish as he showed me love and went out of his way to help me feel secure.

Sometimes when we made love I would cry, feeling the hole in my heart left by his affair. I knew he was in tune with my pain when he began to cry with me. He had the same pain I did, and we were healing the hole together with God's help.

Whenever I feel anxious about our marriage or the future, God reminds me of his purposeful intervention in our lives. I clearly picture the mailman driving away and the bundle of letters sitting on top of the mailbox. Now, in the place of a painful letter, God has delivered Jesus with his gifts of forgiveness, peace, joy and love.

In these moments, I know that God is capable of far more than I could ever ask or imagine in any of life's circumstances. I have finally begun "to grasp how wide and long and high and deep is the love of Christ, and to know this love that surpasses knowledge," and the holes in my heart have been "filled to the measure of all the fullness of God" (Eph 3:18-19).[4]

You Can Experience the Power of Forgiveness

The Bible promises abundant life and peace to all who trust in the principles of godly living. Forgiveness is undeniably the hardest principle to grasp, but it is also the most powerful.

Colossians 3:13 says, "Bear with each other and forgive whatever grievances you may have against one another. Forgive as the Lord forgave you." A courageous dedication to obeying that verse will bring huge benefits in your life. First and foremost, you will have a deeper understanding of Jesus and his love for you. Forgiveness was at the top of his agenda for mankind. When he taught his disciples how to pray he included, "Forgive us our sins, for we also forgive everyone who sins against us" (Lk 11:4). When he was on the cross securing our salvation, he looked down at the people who had brutally mistreated him, and he said, "Father, forgive them, for they do not know what they are doing" (Lk 23:34).

In addition, when you practice forgiveness you will experience freedom from deception and despair. Satan wants to inundate your life with the crippling effects of bitterness and deception. Jesus wants to deliver you by challenging you to walk the pathway of aggressive forgiveness. "For [the Father] has rescued us from the dominion of darkness and brought us into the kingdom of the Son he loves, in whom we have redemption, the forgiveness of sins" (Col 1:13-14).

Forgiving also simplifies your life. Bitterness always complicates. It twists your thinking, your emotional reactions to life and your ability to perform. It dominates your relationships and drains your body of strength. It breeds depression, anxiety and anger. That is why the Bible warns, "See to it that no one misses the grace of God and that no bitter root grows up to cause trouble and defile many" (Heb 12:15).

You make better friends when you are a forgiver. Bitterness breeds its own company, and it doesn't like people who have clear consciences and willing hearts. People who forgive likewise attract people who forgive. Jesus has offered himself to people on earth and teaches them how to forgive from the heart. As you acquire this skill, you too will be more comfortable around those who are free to forgive rather than those who are burdened with bitterness. You will enjoy your life as a child of God. "How great is the love the Father has lavished on us, that we should be called children of God! And that is what we are!" (1 Jn 3:1).

The forgiveness of Christ will bring you eternal freedom, but it will also give you the freedom you need to optimize your everyday life. When you forgive like Jesus, "Then you will know the truth, and the truth will set you free" (Jn 8:32). "So if the Son sets you free, you will be free indeed" (Jn 8:36).

Focus on the Heart
Lord, give me eyes to see the freedom of forgiveness and the bondage of bitterness with equal clarity. Then fill my heart with the courage to always choose forgiveness.

A Step Toward Love
Fill in your name in the following statement of commitment:

I, _____, commit myself today to forgive my spouse for everything he/she may do to offend me. I will not allow the struggles in our relationship to steal my freedom from me.

Notes

Chapter 1: What Is There to Forgive?

[1] "Tales with a Twist," *Reader's Digest*, August 1995, p. 80. Quoted from Paul Rolly and JoAnn Jacobsen-Wells in the Salt Lake *Tribune*.

[2] Rosida Porter, "Musical Car Horn," *Reader's Digest*, March 1994, p. 84.

[3] As told by Sean and Rita.

Chapter 2: Why Should I Forgive?

[1] Judith S. Wallerstein and Sandra Blakslee, *Second Chances* (New York: Ticknor and Fields, 1989), p. 29. The study was a ten-year follow-up study of 131 children from 60 families. They were examined at the time of divorce and again 18 months, 5 years and 10 years after the divorce. Of the initial group of 60 couples, only 2 reconciled!

[2] Ibid.

[3] Ibid., p. 299.

[4] Ibid., p. 308 (words in brackets added).

[5] For more information about the effects of divorce on children see Archibald Hart, *Helping Children Survive Divorce* (Nashville: Word, 1996).

[6] For more information on the process of setting personal boundaries, see Henry Cloud and John Townsend, *Boundaries: When to Say Yes, When to Say No to Take Control of Your Life* (Grand Rapids, Mich.: Zondervan, 1992).

Chapter 7: Reconciling Our Differences

[1] Excerpted from an interview with Joe and Michelle Williams. Their workbook *Reconciling Your Marriage . . . God's Way* was published by Big Valley Grace Community Church in 1997. It is an excellent resource for couples looking to work through the difficult process of reconciliation. Its step-by-step approach is very practical and effective. Copies of the workbook can be obtained from Big Valley Grace Community Church: (209) 577-1604, ext. 248. Or you can write Joe and Michelle at Reconciling God's Way Ministries, 4040 Tully Rd., Modesto, CA 95356.

[2] Ibid., p. 6.

[3] Ibid., p. 28.

[4] Ibid., p. 10.

[5] Ibid., p. 34.

[6] Ibid., p. 37.

[7] For more insight into personality differences see the following resources: David Keirsey and Marilyn Bates, *Please Understand Me: Character & Temperament Types* (Del

Mar, Calif.: Prometheus Nemesis, 1984); Roger R. Pearman with Sarah C. Albritton, *I'm Not Crazy, I'm Just Not You* (Palo Alto, Calif.: Davies-Black, 1997); *Uniquely You*, P.O. Box 490, Blue Ridge, GA 30513, <www.uniquelyyou.com>'; Florence and Marita Littauer, *Personality Puzzle* (Grand Rapids, Mich.: Revell, 1992).

[8]Williams, *Reconciling Your Marriage*, pp. 17, 24.

[9]Ibid., p. 29.

[10]Ibid., p. 34.

Chapter 8: Rebuilding Trust

[1]Michael E. McCullough, Steven J. Sandage and Everett L. Worthington Jr., *To Forgive Is Human* (Downers Grove, Ill.: InterVarsity Press, 1997), p. 151.

In chapters 7 and 8, the authors discuss the importance of forgiveness in the process of our memories. They point out that the mind protects itself from pain in the same way that our bodies protect themselves. As a result, we tell and retell the story of our lives in such a way as to relieve pain. Each time we tell the story we add the nuances of our reaction to the facts this time around. As a result, our memory of our past becomes an "average" picture of each of the times we have told or meditated on the story.

> Once we have an emotional experience, we think about it. We label it, and we recall, not just the mood, not just the visual image, but also the words we used to describe the event to ourselves. As we tell and retell the story to ourselves and to others, we may embellish the story or impoverish it. Before long our memory of the event is changed through retelling. (p. 117)

The bad news is that our memories are not as accurate as we would like to believe. The good news is that we have the ability to modify the story without changing the facts. We can see ourselves as powerful players in the story rather than as victims. We can deliberately build an approach to the story that results in our being victors and conquerors.

Chapter 10: I'm the Only One Who Wants to Work on the Relationship

[1]From a "Dear Abby" column; we have been unable to trace the newspaper or date.

[2]Archibald Hart, *Helping Children Survive Divorce* (Dallas, Tex.: Word, 1996), p. 19.

Chapter 12: The Power of Forgiveness

[1]Taken from an interview with Danna Demetre. Her story is told in *Beneath the Surface* (1996), the story of a couple's journey from selfishness and worldly living to a marriage abandoned to and surrendered to Jesus Christ. Danna now heads up a ministry called Lifestyle Dimensions, 3111 Camino Del Rio North, Suite 203, San Diego, CA 92108. (800) 501-BFIT.

[2]Ibid.

[3]Ibid.

[4]Ibid.